D0826679

1984

George Orwell

SPARK PUBLISHING

SPARKNOTES is a registered trademark of SparkNotes LLC

Spark Publishing
A Division of Barnes & Noble
120 Fifth Avenue
New York, NY 10011
www.sparknotes.com

ISBN-13: 978-1-4114-0324-6
ISBN-10: 1-4114-0324-X

Please submit changes or report errors to www.sparknotes.com/errors.

Printed in the United States.

10 9 8 7 6 5 4 3 2 1

CONTENTS

CONTEXT

BORN ERIC BLAIR IN INDIA IN 1903, George Orwell was educated as a scholarship student at prestigious boarding schools in England. Because of his background—he famously described his family as "lower-upper-middle class"—he never quite fit in, and felt oppressed and outraged by the dictatorial control that the schools he attended exercised over their students' lives. After graduating from Eton, Orwell decided to forego college in order to work as a British Imperial Policeman in Burma. He hated his duties in Burma, where he was required to enforce the strict laws of a political regime he despised. His failing health, which troubled him throughout his life, caused him to return to England on convalescent leave. Once back in England, he quit the Imperial Police and dedicated himself to becoming a writer.

Inspired by Jack London's 1903 book *The People of the Abyss*, which detailed London's experience in the slums of London, Orwell bought ragged clothes from a second-hand store and went to live among the very poor in London. After reemerging, he published a book about this experience, entitled *Down and Out in Paris and London*. He later lived among destitute coal miners in northern England, an experience that caused him to give up on capitalism in favor of democratic socialism. In 1936, he traveled to Spain to report on the Spanish Civil War, where he witnessed firsthand the nightmarish atrocities committed by fascist political regimes. The rise to power of dictators such as Adolf Hitler in Germany and Joseph Stalin in the Soviet Union inspired Orwell's mounting hatred of totalitarianism and political authority. Orwell devoted his energy to writing novels that were politically charged, first with *Animal Farm* in 1945, then with *1984* in 1949.

1984 is one of Orwell's best-crafted novels, and it remains one of the most powerful warnings ever issued against the dangers of a totalitarian society. In Spain, Germany, and the Soviet Union, Orwell had witnessed the danger of absolute political authority in an age of advanced technology. He illustrated that peril harshly in *1984*. Like Aldous Huxley's *Brave New World* (1932), *1984* is one of the most famous novels of the negative utopian, or dystopian, genre. Unlike a utopian novel, in which the writer aims to portray the perfect human society, a novel of negative utopia does the exact opposite: it shows the worst human society imaginable, in an effort to convince readers to avoid any path that might lead toward such societal degradation. In 1949, at the dawn of the nuclear age and before the television had become a fixture in the family home, Orwell's vision of a post-atomic dictatorship in which every individual would be monitored ceaselessly by means of the telescreen seemed terrifyingly possible. That Orwell postulated such a society a mere thirty-five years into the future compounded this fear.

Of course, the world that Orwell envisioned in *1984* did not materialize. Rather than being overwhelmed by totalitarianism, democracy ultimately won out in the Cold War, as seen in the fall of the Berlin Wall and the disintegration of the Soviet Union in the early 1990s. Yet *1984* remains an important novel, in part for the alarm it sounds against the abusive nature of authoritarian governments, but even more so for its penetrating analysis of the psychology of power and the ways that manipulations of language and history can be used as mechanisms of control.

Plot Overview

WINSTON SMITH IS A LOW-RANKING member of the ruling Party in London, in the nation of Oceania. Everywhere Winston goes, even his own home, the Party watches him through telescreens; everywhere he looks he sees the face of the Party's seemingly omniscient leader, a figure known only as Big Brother. The Party controls everything in Oceania, even the people's history and language. Currently, the Party is forcing the implementation of an invented language called Newspeak, which attempts to prevent political rebellion by eliminating all words related to it. Even thinking rebellious thoughts is illegal. Such thoughtcrime is, in fact, the worst of all crimes.

As the novel opens, Winston feels frustrated by the oppression and rigid control of the Party, which prohibits free thought, sex, and any expression of individuality. Winston dislikes the party and has illegally purchased a diary in which to write his criminal thoughts. He has also become fixated on a powerful Party member named O'Brien, whom Winston believes is a secret member of the Brotherhood—the mysterious, legendary group that works to overthrow the Party.

Winston works in the Ministry of Truth, where he alters historical records to fit the needs of the Party. He notices a coworker, a beautiful dark-haired girl, staring at him, and worries that she is an informant who will turn him in for his thoughtcrime. He is troubled by the Party's control of history: the Party claims that Oceania has always been allied with Eastasia in a war against Eurasia, but Winston seems to recall a time when this was not true. The Party also claims that Emmanuel Goldstein, the alleged leader of the Brotherhood, is the most dangerous man alive, but this does not seem plausible to Winston. Winston spends his evenings wandering through the poorest neighborhoods in London, where the proletarians, or proles, live squalid lives, relatively free of Party monitoring.

One day, Winston receives a note from the dark-haired girl that reads "I love you." She tells him her name, Julia, and they begin a covert affair, always on the lookout for signs of Party monitoring. Eventually they rent a room above the secondhand store in the prole district where Winston bought the diary. This relationship lasts for some time. Winston is sure that they will be caught and punished sooner or later (the fatalistic Winston knows that he has been doomed since he wrote his first diary entry), while Julia is more pragmatic and optimistic. As Winston's affair with Julia progresses, his hatred for the Party grows more and more intense. At last, he receives the message that he has been waiting for: O'Brien wants to see him.

Winston and Julia travel to O'Brien's luxurious apartment. As a member of the powerful Inner Party (Winston belongs to the Outer Party), O'Brien leads a life of luxury that Winston can only imagine. O'Brien confirms to Winston and Julia that, like them, he hates the Party, and says that he works against it as a member of the Brotherhood. He indoctrinates Winston and Julia into the Brotherhood, and gives Winston a copy of Emmanuel Goldstein's book, the manifesto of the Brotherhood. Winston reads the book—an amalgam of several forms of class-based twentieth-century social theory—to Julia in the room above the store. Suddenly, soldiers barge in and seize them. Mr. Charrington, the proprietor of the store, is revealed as having been a member of the Thought Police all along.

Torn away from Julia and taken to a place called the Ministry of Love, Winston finds that O'Brien, too, is a Party spy who simply pretended to be a member of the Brotherhood in order to trap Winston into committing an open act of rebellion against the Party. O'Brien spends months torturing and brainwashing Winston, who struggles to resist. At last, O'Brien sends him to the dreaded Room 101, the final destination for anyone who opposes the Party. Here, O'Brien tells Winston that he will be forced to confront his worst fear. Throughout the novel, Winston has had recurring nightmares about rats; O'Brien now straps a cage full of rats onto Winston's head and prepares to allow the rats to eat his face. Winston snaps, pleading with O'Brien to do it to Julia, not to him.

Giving up Julia is what O'Brien wanted from Winston all along. His spirit broken, Winston is released to the outside world. He meets Julia but no longer feels anything for her. He has accepted the Party entirely and has learned to love Big Brother.

CHARACTER LIST

Winston Smith A minor member of the ruling Party in near-future London, Winston Smith is a thin, frail, contemplative, intellectual, and fatalistic thirty-nine-year-old. Winston hates the totalitarian control and enforced repression that are characteristic of his government. He harbors revolutionary dreams.

Julia Winston's lover, a beautiful dark-haired girl working in the Fiction Department at the Ministry of Truth. Julia enjoys sex, and claims to have had affairs with many Party members. Julia is pragmatic and optimistic. Her rebellion against the Party is small and personal, for her own enjoyment, in contrast to Winston's ideological motivation.

O'Brien A mysterious, powerful, and sophisticated member of the Inner Party whom Winston believes is also a member of the Brotherhood, the legendary group of anti-Party rebels.

Big Brother Though he never appears in the novel, and though he may not actually exist, Big Brother, the perceived ruler of Oceania, is an extremely important figure. Everywhere Winston looks he sees posters of Big Brother's face bearing the message "BIG BROTHER IS WATCHING YOU." Big Brother's image is stamped on coins and broadcast on the unavoidable telescreens; it haunts Winston's life and fills him with hatred and fascination.

Mr. Charrington An old man who runs a secondhand store in the prole district. Kindly and encouraging, Mr. Charrington seems to share Winston's interest in the past. He also seems to support Winston's rebellion against the Party and his relationship with Julia, since he rents Winston a room without a telescreen in which to carry out his affair. But Mr. Charrington is not as he seems. He is a member of the Thought Police.

Syme An intelligent, outgoing man who works with Winston at the Ministry of Truth. Syme specializes in language. As the novel opens, he is working on a new edition of the Newspeak dictionary. Winston believes Syme is too intelligent to stay in the Party's favor.

Parsons A fat, obnoxious, and dull Party member who lives near Winston and works at the Ministry of Truth. He has a dull wife and a group of suspicious, ill-mannered children who are members of the Junior Spies.

Emmanuel Goldstein Another figure who exerts an influence on the novel without ever appearing in it. According to the Party, Goldstein is the legendary leader of the Brotherhood. He seems to have been a Party leader who fell out of favor with the regime. In any case, the Party describes him as the most dangerous and treacherous man in Oceania.

ANALYSIS OF MAJOR CHARACTERS

WINSTON SMITH

Orwell's primary goal in *1984* is to demonstrate the terrifying possibilities of totalitarianism. The reader experiences the nightmarish world that Orwell envisions through the eyes of the protagonist, Winston. His personal tendency to resist the stifling of his individuality, and his intellectual ability to reason about his resistance, enables the reader to observe and understand the harsh oppression that the Party, Big Brother, and the Thought Police institute. Whereas Julia is untroubled and somewhat selfish, interested in rebelling only for the pleasures to be gained, Winston is extremely pensive and curious, desperate to understand how and why the Party exercises such absolute power in Oceania. Winston's long reflections give Orwell a chance to explore the novel's important themes, including language as mind control, psychological and physical intimidation and manipulation, and the importance of knowledge of the past.

Apart from his thoughtful nature, Winston's main attributes are his rebelliousness and his fatalism. Winston hates the Party passionately and wants to test the limits of its power; he commits innumerable crimes throughout the novel, ranging from writing "DOWN WITH BIG BROTHER" in his diary, to having an illegal love affair with Julia, to getting himself secretly indoctrinated into the anti-Party Brotherhood. The effort Winston puts into his attempt to achieve freedom and independence ultimately underscores the Party's devastating power. By the end of the novel, Winston's rebellion is revealed as playing into O'Brien's campaign of physical and psychological torture, transforming Winston into a loyal subject of Big Brother.

One reason for Winston's rebellion, and eventual downfall, is his sense of fatalism—his intense (though entirely justified) paranoia about the Party and his overriding belief that the Party will eventually catch and punish him. As soon as he writes "DOWN WITH BIG BROTHER" in his diary, Winston is positive that the Thought Police will quickly capture him for committing a thoughtcrime. Thinking that he is helpless to evade his doom, Winston allows himself to take unnecessary risks, such as trusting O'Brien and renting the room above Mr. Charrington's shop. Deep down, he knows that these risks will increase his chances of being caught by the Party; he even admits this to O'Brien while in prison. But because he believes that he will be caught no matter what he does, he convinces himself that he must continue to rebel. Winston lives in a world in which legitimate optimism is an impossibility; lacking any real hope, he gives himself false hope, fully aware that he is doing so.

JULIA

Julia is Winston's lover and the only other person who Winston can be sure hates the Party and wishes to rebel against it as he does. Whereas Winston is restless, fatalistic, and concerned about large-scale social issues, Julia is sensual, pragmatic, and generally content to live in the moment and make the best of her life. Winston longs to join the Brotherhood and read Emmanuel Goldstein's abstract manifesto; Julia is more concerned with enjoying sex and making practical plans to avoid getting caught by the Party. Winston essentially sees their affair as temporary; his fatalistic attitude makes him unable to imagine his relationship with Julia lasting very long. Julia, on the other hand, is well adapted to her chosen forms of small-scale rebellion. She claims to have had affairs with various Party members, and has no intention of terminating her pleasure seeking, or of being caught (her involvement with Winston is what leads to her capture). Julia is a striking contrast to Winston: apart from their mutual sexual desire and hatred of the Party, most of their traits are dissimilar, if not contradictory.

O'BRIEN

One of the most fascinating aspects of *1984* is the manner in which Orwell shrouds an explicit portrayal of a totalitarian world in an enigmatic aura. While Orwell gives the reader a close look into the personal life of Winston Smith, the reader's only glimpses of Party life are those that Winston himself catches. As a result, many of the Party's inner workings remain unexplained, as do its origins, and the identities and motivations of its leaders. This sense of mystery is centralized in the character of O'Brien, a powerful member of the Inner Party who tricks Winston into believing that he is a member of the revolutionary group called the Brotherhood. O'Brien inducts Winston into the Brotherhood. Later, though, he appears at Winston's jail cell to abuse and brainwash him in the name of the Party. During the process of this punishment, and perhaps as an act of psychological torture, O'Brien admits that he pretended to be connected to the Brotherhood merely to trap Winston in an act of open disloyalty to the Party.

This revelation raises more questions about O'Brien than it answers. Rather than developing as a character throughout the novel, O'Brien actually seems to un-develop: by the end of the book, the reader knows far less about him than they previously had thought. When Winston asks O'Brien if he too has been captured by the Party, O'Brien replies, "They got me long ago." This reply could signify that O'Brien himself was once rebellious, only to be tortured into passive acceptance of the Party. One can also argue that O'Brien pretends to sympathize with Winston merely to gain his trust. Similarly, one cannot be sure whether the Brotherhood actually exists, or if it is simply a Party invention used to trap the disloyal and give the rest of the populace a common enemy. The novel does not answer these questions, but rather leaves O'Brien as a shadowy, symbolic enigma on the fringes of the even more obscure Inner Party.

CHARACTER ANALYSIS

THEMES, MOTIFS & SYMBOLS

THEMES

Themes are the fundamental and often universal ideas explored in a literary work.

THE DANGERS OF TOTALITARIANISM

1984 is a political novel written with the purpose of warning readers in the West of the dangers of totalitarian government. Having witnessed firsthand the horrific lengths to which totalitarian governments in Spain and Russia would go in order to sustain and increase their power, Orwell designed *1984* to sound the alarm in Western nations still unsure about how to approach the rise of communism. In 1949, the Cold War had not yet escalated, many American intellectuals supported communism, and the state of diplomacy between democratic and communist nations was highly ambiguous. In the American press, the Soviet Union was often portrayed as a great moral experiment. Orwell, however, was deeply disturbed by the widespread cruelties and oppressions he observed in communist countries, and seems to have been particularly concerned by the role of technology in enabling oppressive governments to monitor and control their citizens.

In *1984*, Orwell portrays the perfect totalitarian society, the most extreme realization imaginable of a modern-day government with absolute power. The title of the novel was meant to indicate to its readers in 1949 that the story represented a real possibility for the near future: if totalitarianism were not opposed, the title suggested, some variation of the world described in the novel could become a reality in only thirty-five years. Orwell portrays a state in which government monitors and controls every aspect of human life to the extent that even having a disloyal thought is against the law. As the novel progresses, the timidly rebellious Winston Smith sets out to challenge the limits of the Party's power, only to discover that its ability to control and enslave its subjects dwarfs even his most paranoid conceptions of its reach. As the reader comes to understand through Winston's eyes, The Party uses a number of techniques to control its citizens, each of which is an important theme of its own in the novel. These include:

PSYCHOLOGICAL MANIPULATION
The Party barrages its subjects with psychological stimuli designed to overwhelm the mind's capacity for independent thought. The giant telescreen in every citizen's room blasts a constant stream of propaganda designed to make the failures and shortcomings of the Party appear to be triumphant successes. The telescreens also monitor behavior—everywhere they go, citizens are continuously reminded, especially by means of the omnipresent signs reading "BIG BROTHER IS WATCHING YOU," that the authorities are scrutinizing them. The Party undermines family structure by inducting children into an organization called the Junior Spies, which brainwashes and encourages them to spy on their parents and report any instance of disloyalty to the Party. The Party also forces individuals to suppress their sexual desires, treating sex as merely a procreative duty whose end is the creation of new Party members. The Party then channels people's pent-up frustration and emotion into intense, ferocious displays of hatred against the Party's political enemies. Many of these enemies have been invented by the Party expressly for this purpose.

PHYSICAL CONTROL
In addition to manipulating their minds, the Party also controls the bodies of its subjects. The Party constantly watches for any sign of disloyalty, to the point that, as Winston observes, even a tiny facial twitch could lead to an arrest. A person's own nervous system becomes his greatest enemy. The Party forces its members to undergo mass morning exercises called the Physical Jerks, and then to work long, grueling days at government agencies, keeping people in a general state of exhaustion. Anyone who does manage to defy the Party is punished and "reeducated" through systematic and brutal torture. After being subjected to weeks of this intense treatment, Winston himself comes to the conclusion that nothing is more powerful than physical pain—no emotional loyalty or moral conviction can overcome it. By conditioning the minds of their victims with physical torture, the Party is able to control reality, convincing its subjects that $2 + 2 = 5$.

THEMES

CONTROL OF INFORMATION AND HISTORY

The Party controls every source of information, managing and re-writing the content of all newspapers and histories for its own ends. The Party does not allow individuals to keep records of their past, such as photographs or documents. As a result, memories become fuzzy and unreliable, and citizens become perfectly willing to believe whatever the Party tells them. By controlling the present, the Party is able to manipulate the past. And in controlling the past, the Party can justify all of its actions in the present.

TECHNOLOGY

By means of telescreens and hidden microphones across the city, the Party is able to monitor its members almost all of the time. Additionally, the Party employs complicated mechanisms (*1984* was written in the era before computers) to exert large-scale control on economic production and sources of information, and fearsome machinery to inflict torture upon those it deems enemies. *1984* reveals that technology, which is generally perceived as working toward moral good, can also facilitate the most diabolical evil.

LANGUAGE AS MIND CONTROL

One of Orwell's most important messages in *1984* is that language is of central importance to human thought because it structures and limits the ideas that individuals are capable of formulating and expressing. If control of language were centralized in a political agency, Orwell proposes, such an agency could possibly alter the very structure of language to make it impossible to even conceive of disobedient or rebellious thoughts, because there would be no words with which to think them. This idea manifests itself in the language of Newspeak, which the Party has introduced to replace English. The Party is constantly refining and perfecting Newspeak, with the ultimate goal that no one will be capable of conceptualizing anything that might question the Party's absolute power.

Interestingly, many of Orwell's ideas about language as a con-trolling force have been modified by writers and critics seeking to deal with the legacy of colonialism. During colonial times, foreign powers took political and military control of distant regions and, as a part of their occupation, instituted their own language as the language of government and business. Postcolonial writers often analyze or redress the damage done to local populations by the loss of language and the attendant loss of culture and historical connection.

Motifs

Motifs are recurring structures, contrasts, and literary devices that can help to develop and inform the text's major themes.

Doublethink

The idea of "doublethink" emerges as an important consequence of the Party's massive campaign of large-scale psychological manipulation. Simply put, doublethink is the ability to hold two contradictory ideas in one's mind at the same time. As the Party's mind-control techniques break down an individual's capacity for independent thought, it becomes possible for that individual to believe anything that the Party tells them, even while possessing information that runs counter to what they are being told. At the Hate Week rally, for instance, the Party shifts its diplomatic allegiance, so the nation it has been at war with suddenly becomes its ally, and its former ally becomes its new enemy. When the Party speaker suddenly changes the nation he refers to as an enemy in the middle of his speech, the crowd accepts his words immediately, and is ashamed to find that it has made the wrong signs for the event. In the same way, people are able to accept the Party ministries' names, though they contradict their functions: the Ministry of Plenty oversees economic shortages, the Ministry of Peace wages war, the Ministry of Truth conducts propaganda and historical revisionism, and the Ministry of Love is the center of the Party's operations of torture and punishment.

Urban Decay

Urban decay proves a pervasive motif in *1984*. The London that Winston Smith calls home is a dilapidated, rundown city in which buildings are crumbling, conveniences such as elevators never work, and necessities such as electricity and plumbing are extremely unreliable. Though Orwell never discusses the theme openly, it is clear that the shoddy disintegration of London, just like the widespread hunger and poverty of its inhabitants, is due to the Party's mismanagement and incompetence. One of the themes of *1984*, inspired by the history of twentieth-century communism, is that totalitarian regimes are viciously effective at enhancing their own power and miserably incompetent at providing for their citizens. The grimy urban decay in London is an important visual reminder of this idea, and offers insight into the Party's priorities through its contrast to the immense technology the Party develops to spy on its citizens.

SYMBOLS

> *Symbols are objects, characters, figures, and colors used to represent abstract ideas or concepts.*

BIG BROTHER

Throughout London, Winston sees posters showing a man gazing down over the words "BIG BROTHER IS WATCHING YOU" everywhere he goes. Big Brother is the face of the Party. The citizens are told that he is the leader of the nation and the head of the Party, but Winston can never determine whether or not he actually exists. In any case, the face of Big Brother symbolizes the Party in its public manifestation; he is a reassurance to most people (the warmth of his name suggests his ability to protect), but he is also an open threat (one cannot escape his gaze). Big Brother also symbolizes the vagueness with which the higher ranks of the Party present themselves—it is impossible to know who really rules Oceania, what life is like for the rulers, or why they act as they do. Winston thinks he remembers that Big Brother emerged around 1960, but the Party's official records date Big Brother's existence back to 1930, before Winston was even born.

THE GLASS PAPERWEIGHT AND ST. CLEMENT'S CHURCH

By deliberately weakening people's memories and flooding their minds with propaganda, the Party is able to replace individuals' memories with its own version of the truth. It becomes nearly impossible for people to question the Party's power in the present when they accept what the Party tells them about the past—that the Party arose to protect them from bloated, oppressive capitalists, and that the world was far uglier and harsher before the Party came to power. Winston vaguely understands this principle. He struggles to recover his own memories and formulate a larger picture of what has happened to the world. Winston buys a paperweight in an antique store in the prole district that comes to symbolize his attempt to reconnect with the past. Symbolically, when the Thought Police arrest Winston at last, the paperweight shatters on the floor.

The old picture of St. Clement's Church in the room that Winston rents above Mr. Charrington's shop is another representation of the lost past. Winston associates a song with the picture that ends with the words "Here comes the chopper to chop off your head!" This is an important foreshadow, as it is the telescreen hidden behind the

SYMBOLS

picture that ultimately leads the Thought Police to Winston, symbolizing the Party's corrupt control of the past.

THE PLACE WHERE THERE IS NO DARKNESS
Throughout the novel Winston imagines meeting O'Brien in "the place where there is no darkness." The words first come to him in a dream, and he ponders them for the rest of the novel. Eventually, Winston does meet O'Brien in the place where there is no darkness; instead of being the paradise Winston imagined, it is merely a prison cell in which the light is never turned off. The idea of "the place where there is no darkness" symbolizes Winston's approach to the future: possibly because of his intense fatalism (he believes that he is doomed no matter what he does), he unwisely allows himself to trust O'Brien, even though inwardly he senses that O'Brien might be a Party operative.

THE TELESCREENS
The omnipresent telescreens are the book's most visible symbol of the Party's constant monitoring of its subjects. In their dual capability to blare constant propaganda and observe citizens, the telescreens also symbolize how totalitarian government abuses technology for its own ends instead of exploiting its knowledge to improve civilization.

THE RED-ARMED PROLE WOMAN
The red-armed prole woman whom Winston hears singing through the window represents Winston's one legitimate hope for the long-term future: the possibility that the proles will eventually come to recognize their plight and rebel against the Party. Winston sees the prole woman as a prime example of reproductive virility; he often imagines her giving birth to the future generations that will finally challenge the Party's authority.

Summary & Analysis

Book One: Chapter I

Summary: Chapter I

On a cold day in April of 1984, a man named Winston Smith returns to his home, a dilapidated apartment building called Victory Mansions. Thin, frail, and thirty-nine years old, it is painful for him to trudge up the stairs because he has a varicose ulcer above his right ankle. The elevator is always out of service so he does not try to use it. As he climbs the staircase, he is greeted on each landing by a poster depicting an enormous face, underscored by the words "BIG BROTHER IS WATCHING YOU."

Winston is an insignificant official in the Party, the totalitarian political regime that rules all of Airstrip One—the land that used to be called England—as part of the larger state of Oceania. Though Winston is technically a member of the ruling class, his life is still under the Party's oppressive political control. In his apartment, an instrument called a telescreen—which is always on, spouting propaganda, and through which the Thought Police are known to monitor the actions of citizens—shows a dreary report about pig iron. Winston keeps his back to the screen. From his window he sees the Ministry of Truth, where he works as a propaganda officer altering historical records to match the Party's official version of past events. Winston thinks about the other Ministries that exist as part of the Party's governmental apparatus: the Ministry of Peace, which wages war; the Ministry of Plenty, which plans economic shortages; and the dreaded Ministry of Love, the center of the Inner Party's loathsome activities.

> *WAR IS PEACE*
> *FREEDOM IS SLAVERY*
> *IGNORANCE IS STRENGTH*
> *(See* QUOTATIONS, *p. 43)*

From a drawer in a little alcove hidden from the telescreen, Winston pulls out a small diary he recently purchased. He found the diary in a secondhand store in the proletarian district, where the very poor live relatively unimpeded by Party monitoring. The *proles*, as they are called, are so impoverished and insignificant that the Party does not consider them a threat to its power. Winston begins to write in his diary, although he realizes that this constitutes an act of rebellion against the Party. He describes the films he watched the night before. He thinks about his lust and hatred for a dark-haired girl who works in the Fiction Department at the Ministry of Truth, and about an important Inner Party member named O'Brien—a man he is sure is an enemy of the Party. Winston remembers the moment before that day's Two Minutes Hate, an assembly during which Party orators whip the populace into a frenzy of hatred against the enemies of Oceania. Just before the Hate began, Winston knew he hated Big Brother, and saw the same loathing in O'Brien's eyes.

Winston looks down and realizes that he has written "DOWN WITH BIG BROTHER" over and over again in his diary. He has committed thoughtcrime—the most unpardonable crime—and he knows that the Thought Police will seize him sooner or later. Just then, there is a knock at the door.

ANALYSIS: CHAPTER I

The first few chapters of 1984 are devoted to introducing the major characters and themes of the novel. These chapters also acquaint the reader with the harsh and oppressive world in which the novel's protagonist, Winston Smith, lives. It is from Winston's perspective that the reader witnesses the brutal physical and psychological cruelties wrought upon the people by their government. Orwell's main goals in 1984 are to depict the frightening techniques a totalitarian government (in which a single ruling class possesses absolute power) might use to control its subjects, and to illustrate the extent of the control that government is able to exert. To this end, Orwell offers a protagonist who has been subject to Party control all of his life, but who has arrived at a dim idea of rebellion and freedom.

Unlike virtually anyone else in Airstrip One, Winston seems to understand that he might be happier if he were free. Orwell emphasizes the fact that, in the world of Airstrip One, freedom is a shocking and alien notion: simply writing in a diary—an act of self-expression—is an unpardonable crime. He also highlights the extent of government control by describing how the Party watches its members through the giant telescreens in their homes. The panic that grabs hold of Winston when he realizes that he has written "DOWN WITH BIG BROTHER" evidences his certainty in the pervasive omniscience of the Party and in the efficiency of its monitoring techniques.

Winston's diary entry, his first overt act of rebellion, is the primary plot development in this chapter. It illustrates Winston's desire, however slight, to break free of the Party's total control. Winston's hatred of Party oppression has been festering for some time, possibly even for most of his life. It is important to note that the novel, however, opens on the day that this hatred finds an active expression—Winston's instinct to rebel singles him out of the sheeplike masses. Unlike the rest of the general public who do not find the Party's contradictions problematic, Winston is aware of himself as an entity separate from the totalitarian state. He realizes that writing in the diary has altered his life irrevocably and that he is no longer simply another citizen of Oceania. In writing in the diary he becomes a thought-criminal, and he considers himself doomed from the very start: "Thoughtcrime was not a thing that could be concealed forever . . . Sooner or later they were bound to get you."

One of the most important themes of *1984* is governmental use of psychological manipulation and physical control as a means of maintaining its power. This theme is present in Chapter I, as Winston's grasping at freedom illustrates the terrifying extent to which citizens are not in control of their own minds. The telescreens in their homes blare out a constant stream of propaganda, touting the greatness of Oceania and the success of the Party in ruling it. Each day citizens are required to attend the Two Minutes Hate, an intense mass rally in which they are primed with fury and hatred for Oceania's rival nations, venting their own pent-up emotions in the process. The government, meanwhile, expresses its role in an outlandishly dishonest fashion, as seen in the stark contradiction between the name and function of each of its ministries. The net effect of this psychological manipulation is a complete breakdown of the independence of an individual's mind. Independence and will are replaced by a fear of, and faith in, the Party; indeed, individual thought has become so alien the population accepts that the Party has made it a crime.

BOOK ONE: CHAPTERS II–III

SUMMARY: CHAPTER II

Winston opens the door fearfully, assuming that the Thought Police have arrived to arrest him for writing in the diary. However, it is only Mrs. Parsons, a neighbor in his apartment building, needing help with the plumbing while her husband is away. In Mrs. Parsons's apartment, Winston is tormented by the fervent Parsons children, who, being Junior Spies, accuse him of thoughtcrime. The Junior Spies is an organization of children who monitor adults for disloyalty to the Party, and frequently succeed in catching them—Mrs. Parsons herself seems afraid of her zealous children. The children are very agitated because their mother won't let them go to a public hanging of some of the Party's political enemies in the park that evening. Back in his apartment, Winston remembers a dream in which a man's voice—O'Brien's, he thinks—said to him, "We shall meet in the place where there is no darkness." Winston writes in his diary that his thoughtcrime makes him a dead man, then he hides the book.

SUMMARY: CHAPTER III

Winston dreams of being with his mother on a sinking ship. He feels strangely responsible for his mother's disappearance in a political purge almost twenty years ago. He then dreams of a place called The Golden Country, where the dark-haired girl takes off her clothes and runs toward him in an act of freedom that annihilates the whole Party. He wakes with the word "Shakespeare" on his lips, not knowing where it came from. A high-pitched whistle sounds from the telescreen, a signal that office workers must wake up. It is time for the Physical Jerks, a round of grotesque exercise.

As he exercises, Winston thinks about his childhood, which he barely remembers. Having no physical records such as photographs and documents, he thinks, makes one's life lose its outline in one's memory. Winston considers Oceania's relationship to the other countries in the world, Eurasia and Eastasia. According to official history, Oceania has always been at war with Eurasia and in alliance with Eastasia, but Winston knows that the records have been changed. Winston remembers that no one had heard of Big Brother, the leader of the Party, before 1960, but stories about him now appear in histories going back to the 1930s.

As Winston has these thoughts, a voice from the telescreen suddenly calls out his name, reprimanding him for not working hard enough at the Physical Jerks. Winston breaks out into a hot sweat and tries harder to touch his toes.

ANALYSIS: CHAPTERS II–III

Winston's fatalism is a central component of his character. He has been fearing the power of the Party for decades, and the guilt he feels after having committed a crime against the Party overwhelms him, rendering him absolutely certain that he will be caught and punished. Winston only occasionally allows himself to feel any hope for the future. His general pessimism not only reflects the social conditioning against which Orwell hopes to warn his readers, but also casts a general gloom on the novel's atmosphere; it makes a dark world seem even darker.

An important aspect of the Party's oppression of its subjects is the forced repression of sexual appetite. Initially, Winston must confine his sexual desires to the realm of fantasy, as when he dreams in Chapter II of an imaginary Golden Country in which he makes love to the dark-haired girl. Like sex in general, the dark-haired girl is treated as an unfathomable mystery in this section; she is someone whom Winston simultaneously desires and distrusts with a profound paranoia.

The Party's control of the past is another significant component of its psychological control over its subjects: that no one is allowed to keep physical records documenting the past prevents people from challenging the government's motivations, actions, and authority. Winston only vaguely remembers a time before the Party came to power, and memories of his past enter his mind only in dreams, which are the most secure repositories for thoughts, feelings, and memories that must be suppressed in waking life.

Winston's dreams are also prophetic, foreshadowing future events. Winston will indeed make love to the dark-haired girl in an idyllic country landscape. The same is true for his dream of O'Brien, in which he hears O'Brien's voice promise to meet him "in the place where there is no darkness." At the end of the novel, Winston will indeed meet O'Brien in a place without darkness, but that place will be nothing like what Winston expects. The phrase "the place where there is no darkness" recurs throughout the novel, and it orients Winston toward his future.

An important motif that emerges in the first three chapters of 1984 is that of urban decay. Under the supposedly benign guidance of the Party, London has fallen apart. Winston's world is a nasty, brutish place to live—conveniences are mostly out of order and buildings are ramshackle and unsafe. In contrast to the broken elevator in

Winston's rundown apartment building, the presence of the technologically advanced telescreen illustrates the Party's prioritization of strict control and utter neglect of citizens' quality of living.

Winston's encounter with the Parsons children in Chapter II demonstrates the Party's influence on family life. Children are effectively converted into spies and trained to watch the actions of their parents with extreme suspicion. The fear Mrs. Parsons shows for her children foreshadows Winston's encounter in jail with her husband, who is turned in to the Party by his own child for committing thoughtcrime. Orwell was inspired in his creation of the Junior Spies by a real organization called Hitler Youth that thrived in Nazi Germany. This group instilled a fanatic patriotism in children that led them to such behaviors as monitoring their parents for any sign of deviation from Nazi orthodoxy, in much the same manner that Orwell later ascribed to the Junior Spies.

BOOK ONE: CHAPTERS IV–VI

SUMMARY: CHAPTER IV

Winston goes to his job in the Records section of the Ministry of Truth, where he works with a "speakwrite" (a machine that types as he dictates into it) and destroys obsolete documents. He updates Big Brother's orders and Party records so that they match new developments—Big Brother can never be wrong. Even when the citizens of Airstrip One are forced to live with less food, they are told that they are being given more than ever and, by and large, they believe it. This day, Winston must alter the record of a speech made in December 1983, which referred to Comrade Withers, one of Big Brother's former officials who has since been vaporized. Since Comrade Withers was executed as an enemy of the Party, it is unacceptable to have a document on file praising him as a loyal Party member.

Winston invents a person named Comrade Ogilvy and substitutes him for Comrade Withers in the records. Comrade Ogilvy, though a product of Winston's imagination, is an ideal Party man, opposed to sex and suspicious of everyone. Comrade Withers has become an "unperson:" he has ceased to exist. Watching a man named Comrade Tillotson in the cubicle across the way, Winston reflects on the activity in the Ministry of Truth, where thousands of workers correct the flow of history to make it match party ideology, and churn out endless drivel—even pornography—to pacify the brutally destitute proletariat.

SUMMARY: CHAPTER V

Winston has lunch with a man named Syme, an intelligent Party member who works on a revised dictionary of Newspeak, the official language of Oceania. Syme tells Winston that Newspeak aims to narrow the range of thought to render thoughtcrime impossible. If there are no words in a language that are capable of expressing independent, rebellious thoughts, no one will ever be able to rebel, or even to conceive of the idea of rebellion. Winston thinks that Syme's intelligence will get him vaporized one day. Parsons, a pudgy and fervent Party official and the husband of the woman whose plumbing Winston fixed in Chapter II, comes into the canteen and elicits a contribution from Winston for neighborhood Hate Week. He apologizes to Winston for his children's harassment the day before, but is openly proud of their spirit.

Suddenly, an exuberant message from the Ministry of Plenty announces increases in production over the loudspeakers. Winston reflects that the alleged increase in the chocolate ration to twenty grams was actually a reduction from the day before, but those around him seem to accept the announcement joyfully and without suspicion. Winston feels that he is being watched; he looks up and sees the dark-haired girl staring at him. He worries again that she is a Party agent.

SUMMARY: CHAPTER VI

That evening, Winston records in his diary his memory of his last sexual encounter, which was with a prole prostitute. He thinks about the Party's hatred of sex, and decides that their goal is to remove pleasure from the sexual act, so that it becomes merely a duty to the Party, a way of producing new Party members. Winston's former wife Katherine hated sex, and as soon as they realized they would never have children, they separated.

Winston desperately wants to have an enjoyable sexual affair, which he sees as the ultimate act of rebellion. In his diary, he writes that the prole prostitute was old and ugly, but that he went through with the sex act anyway. He realizes that recording the act in his diary hasn't alleviated his anger, depression, or rebellion. He still longs to shout profanities at the top of his voice.

ANALYSIS: CHAPTERS IV–VI

Winston's life at work in the sprawling Ministry of Truth illustrates the world of the Party in operation—calculated propaganda, altered records, revised history—and demonstrates the effects of such deleterious mechanisms on Winston's mind. The idea of doublethink—explained in Chapter III as the ability to believe and disbelieve simultaneously in the same idea, or to believe in two contradictory ideas simultaneously—provides the psychological key to the Party's control of the past. Doublethink allows the citizens under Party control to accept slogans like "War is peace" and "Freedom is slavery," and enables the workers at the Ministry of Truth to believe in the false versions of the records that they themselves have altered. With the belief of the workers, the records become functionally true. Winston struggles under the weight of this oppressive machinery, and yearns to be able to trust his own memory.

Accompanying the psychological aspect of the Party's oppression is the physical aspect. Winston realizes that his own nervous system has become his archenemy. The condition of being constantly monitored and having to repress every feeling and instinct forces Winston to maintain self-control at all costs; even a facial twitch suggesting struggle could lead to arrest, demonstrating the thoroughness of the Party's control. This theme of control through physical monitoring culminates with Winston's realization toward the end of the book that nothing in human experience is worse than the feeling of physical pain.

Winston's repressed sexuality—one of his key reasons for despising the Party and wanting to rebel—becomes his overt concern in Chapter VI, when he remembers his last encounter with a prole prostitute. The dingy, nasty memory makes Winston desperate to have an enjoyable, authentic erotic experience. He thinks that the Party's "real, undeclared purpose was to remove all pleasure from the sexual act." Sex can be seen as the ultimate act of individualism, as a representation of ultimate emotional and physical pleasure, and for its roots in the individual's desire to continue himself or herself through reproduction. By transforming sex into a duty, the Party strikes another psychological blow against individualism: under Big Brother's regime, the goal of sex is not to reproduce one's individual genes, but simply to create new members of the Party.

BOOK ONE: CHAPTERS VII–VIII

SUMMARY: CHAPTER VII

Winston writes in his diary that any hope for revolution against the Party must come from the proles. He believes that the Party cannot be destroyed from within, and that even the Brotherhood, a legend-ary revolutionary group, lacks the wherewithal to defeat the mighty Thought Police. The proles, on the other hand make up eighty-five percent of the population of Oceania, and could easily muster the strength and manpower to overcome the Police. However, the pro-les lead brutish, ignorant, animalistic lives, and lack both the energy and interest to revolt; most of them do not even understand that the Party is oppressing them.

Winston looks through a children's history book to get a feeling for what has really happened in the world. The Party claims to have built ideal cities, but London, where Winston lives, is a wreck: the electricity seldom works, buildings decay, and people live in poverty and fear. Lacking a reliable official record, Winston does not know what to think about the past. The Party's claims that it has increased the literacy rate, reduced the infant mortality rate, and given every-one better food and shelter could all be fantasy. Winston suspects that these claims are untrue, but he has no way to know for sure, since history has been written entirely by the Party.

> In the end the Party would announce that two and two
> made five, and you would have to believe it.
> (See QUOTATIONS, p. 44)

Winston remembers an occasion when he caught the Party in a lie. In the mid-1960s, a cultural backlash caused the original leaders of the Revolution to be arrested. One day, Winston saw a few of these deposed leaders sitting at the Chestnut Tree Café, a gathering place for out-of-favor Party members. A song played—"Under the spreading chestnut tree / I sold you and you sold me"—and one of the Party members, Rutherford, began to weep. Winston never for-got the incident, and one day came upon a photograph that proved that the Party members had been in New York at the time that they were allegedly committing treason in Eurasia. Terrified, Winston destroyed the photograph, but it remains embedded in his memory as a concrete example of Party dishonesty.

Winston thinks of his writing in his diary as a kind of letter to O'Brien. Though Winston knows almost nothing about O'Brien be-yond his name, he is sure that he detects a strain of independence and rebellion in him, a consciousness of oppression similar to Winston's own. Thinking about the Party's control of every record of the truth, Winston realizes that the Party requires its members to deny the evidence of their eyes and ears. He believes that true freedom lies in the ability to interpret reality as one perceives it, to be able to say "2 + 2 = 4."

SUMMARY: CHAPTER VIII

> *When memory failed and written records were falsified ...*
> *(See* QUOTATIONS, *p. 45)*

Winston goes for a walk through the prole district, and envies the simple lives of the common people. He enters a pub where he sees an old man—a possible link to the past. He talks to the old man and tries to ascertain whether, in the days before the Party, people were really exploited by bloated capitalists, as the Party records claim. The old man's memory is too vague to provide an answer. Winston laments that the past has been left to the proles, who will inevitably forget it.

Winston walks to the secondhand store in which he bought the diary and buys a clear glass paperweight with a pink coral center from Mr. Charrington, the proprietor. Mr. Charrington takes him upstairs to a private room with no telescreen, where a print of St. Clement's Church looks down from the wall, evoking the old rhyme: "Oranges and lemons, say the bells of St. Clement's / You owe me three farthings, say the bells of St. Martin's."

On the way home, Winston sees a figure in blue Party overalls—the dark-haired girl, apparently following him. Terrified, he imagines hitting her with a cobblestone or with the paperweight in his pocket. He hurries home and decides that the best thing to do is to commit suicide before the Party catches him. He realizes that if the Thought Police catch him, they will torture him before they kill him. He tries to calm himself by thinking about O'Brien and about the place where there is no darkness that O'Brien mentioned in Winston's dreams. Troubled, he takes a coin from his pocket and looks into the face of Big Brother. He cannot help but recall the Party slogans: "WAR IS PEACE," "FREEDOM IS SLAVERY," "IGNORANCE IS STRENGTH."

ANALYSIS: CHAPTERS VI–VII

After a trio of chapters devoted largely to the work life of minor Party members, Orwell shifts the focus to the world of the very poor. The most important plot development in this section comes with Winston's visit to Mr. Charrington's antiques shop, which stands as a veritable museum of the past in relation to the rest of

Winston's history-deprived world. The theme of the importance of having knowledge about the past in order to understand the present is heavily emphasized here. Orwell demonstrates how the Party, by controlling history, forces its members into lives of uncertainty, ignorance, and total reliance upon the Party for all of the information necessary to function in the world.

Winston's trip to the prole district illustrates the relationship between social class and awareness of one's situation. Life in the prole district is animalistic, filthy, and impoverished. The proles have greater freedom than minor Party members such as Winston, but lack the awareness to use or appreciate that freedom. Winston's desire to attain a unilateral, abstract understanding of the Party's methods and evils in order to consider and reject them epitomizes his speculative, restless nature. He obsesses about history in particular, trying to understand how the Party's control of information about the past enhances its power in the present. In contrast, the old man in the bar whom Winston addresses is too concerned with his bladder and feet to remember the past, and has no sense of the Party's impact on his life. Winston knows that the Party does not "reeducate" the proles because it believes the proles to be too unintelligent to pose a threat to the government. Nevertheless, Winston believes that the proles hold the key to the past and, hence, to the future.

Like Winston's dream phrase "the place where there is no darkness," which reappears in Chapter VIII, the picture of St. Clement's Church hanging in Mr. Charrington's upstairs room functions as a motif tied to Winston's fruitless hope. Like the paperweight, an important symbol of Winston's dreams of freedom, the picture represents Winston's desire to make a connection with a past that the Party has suppressed. However, his attempt to appropriate the past as a means of exposing the Party, like his attempt to appropriate the room as a safe harbor for his disloyalty, is ultimately thwarted by the Party's mechanisms. The phrase associated with the picture ends on an ominous note—"Here comes a chopper to chop off your head." This rhyme foreshadows the connection between the picture (behind which a telescreen is hidden) and the termination of Winston's private rebellion.

BOOK TWO: CHAPTERS I–III

SUMMARY: CHAPTER I

At work one morning, Winston walks toward the men's room and notices the dark-haired girl with her arm in a sling. She falls, and when Winston helps her up, she passes him a note that reads "I love you." Winston tries desperately to figure out the note's meaning. He has long suspected that the dark-haired girl is a political spy monitoring his behavior, but now she claims to love him. Before Winston can fully comprehend this development, Parsons interrupts him with talk about his preparations for Hate Week. The note from the dark-haired girl makes Winston feel a sudden, powerful desire to live.

After several days of nervous tension during which he does not speak to her, Winston manages to sit at the same lunchroom table as the girl. They look down as they converse to avoid being noticed, and plan a meeting in Victory Square where they will be able to hide from the telescreens amid the movement of the crowds. They meet in the square and witness a convoy of Eurasian prisoners being tormented by a venomous crowd. The girl gives Winston directions to a place where they can have their tryst, instructing him to take a train from Paddington Station to the countryside. They manage to hold hands briefly.

SUMMARY: CHAPTER II

Executing their plan, Winston and the girl meet in the country. Though he has no idea what to expect, Winston no longer believes that the dark-haired girl is a spy. He worries that there might be microphones hidden in the bushes, but feels reassured by the dark-haired girl's evident experience. She tells him that her name is Julia, and tears off her Junior Anti-Sex League sash. Winston becomes aroused when they move into the woods, and they make love; the experience is nearly identical to the passionate sexual encounter about which Winston has dreamed. Afterward, Winston asks Julia if she has done this before, and she replies that she has—scores of times. Thrilled, he tells her that the more men she has been with, the more he loves her, since it means that more Party members are committing crimes.

SUMMARY: CHAPTER III

The next morning, Julia makes the practical preparations for their return to London, and she and Winston head back to their normal lives. Over the coming weeks, they arrange several brief meetings in the city. At a rendezvous in a ruined church, Julia tells Winston about living in a hostel with thirty other girls, and about her first illicit sexual encounter. Unlike Winston, Julia is not interested in widespread rebellion; she simply likes outwitting the party and enjoying herself. She explains to Winston that the Party prohibits sex in order to channel the sexual frustration of the citizenry into fervent opposition to Party enemies and impassioned worship of Big Brother.

Winston tells Julia about a walk he once took with his ex-wife Katherine, during which he thought about pushing her off of a cliff. He says that it would not have mattered whether he pushed her or not, because it is impossible to win against the forces of oppression that govern their lives.

ANALYSIS: CHAPTERS I–III

Like the Two Minutes Hate, the Party's parading of political enemies through public squares is a demonstration of psychological manipulation. The convoy channels the public's hatred away from the Party into a political direction that is helpful to the Party. Additionally, the Party's use of such displays illustrates how war serves to preserve cultural uniformity. War unites the citizens in opposition against some shadowy foreign evil while also making it impossible for its subjects to meet or exchange ideas with citizens from other countries, since the only foreigners in London are prisoners of war. In concert with the Party's rewriting of history, this policy leaves Oceania's inhabitants with nothing against which to compare their lives, rendering them unable to challenge the status quo.

The opening of Book Two, in which Winston meets Julia and begins the erotic affair he has so deeply desired, commences the main section of the novel and strikes an immediate contrast between the two lovers. Unlike Winston, Julia is neither overly speculative about, nor troubled by, the Party. Rather, she possesses a mix of sensuality and practicality that enables her to plan their affair with ruthless efficiency and then enjoy it with abandon. Julia also lacks Winston's fatalism. When he tells her, "We are the dead," she replies calmly, "We're not dead yet." Julia is more optimistic than Winston, and uses her body to remind him that he is alive. She accepts the Party and her life for what it is, and tries to make the best of a situation that cannot be greatly improved.

Though not interested in Winston's need to understand the Party, Julia does facilitate Winston's attempts to undermine the Party. In Chapter III, she produces some of the most astute analysis of the Party in the novel. Her understanding of sexual repression as a mechanism to incite "war fever" and "leader worship" renders her sexual activity a political act. From Winston's point of view, the significance of having unauthorized sex with another Party member lies in the fact that his rebellion is no longer confined to himself. Though he considers her somewhat self-absorbed, Winston is thrilled that Julia has had so many affairs with so many Party members. Sexual jealousy no longer has a place, as Winston revels in the possibility of widespread rebellion against the Party's strict mandates.

BOOK TWO: CHAPTERS IV–VI

SUMMARY: CHAPTER IV

Winston looks around the little room above Mr. Charrington's shop, which he has rented—foolishly, he thinks—for his affair with Julia. Outside, a burly, red-armed woman sings a song and hangs up her laundry. Winston and Julia have been busy with the city's preparations for Hate Week, and Winston has been frustrated by their inability to meet. The problem was exacerbated by the fact that Julia has had her period. Winston wishes that he and Julia could lead a more leisurely, romantic life, like an old, married couple.

Julia comes into the room with sugar, coffee, and bread—luxuries only members of the Inner Party could normally obtain. She puts on makeup, and her beauty and femininity overwhelm Winston. Lounging in bed in the evening, Julia sees a rat; Winston, afraid of rats more than anything else, is horrified. Julia looks through the room, and notices the paperweight. Winston tells her that the paperweight is a link to the past. They sing the song about St. Clement's Church, and Julia says that one day she will clean the old picture of the church. When Julia leaves, Winston sits gazing into the crystal paperweight, imagining living inside it with Julia in an eternal stasis.

SUMMARY: CHAPTER V

As Winston predicted would happen, Syme vanishes. During the preparations for Hate Week, the city comes alive with the heat of the summer, and even the proles seem rowdy. Parsons hangs streamers everywhere and his children sing a new song, called "Hate Song," written in celebration of the event. Winston becomes increasingly obsessed with the room above Mr. Charrington's shop, thinking about it even when he cannot go there. He fantasizes that Katherine will die, which would allow him to marry Julia; he even dreams of altering his identity to become a prole. Winston and Julia talk about the Brotherhood; he tells her about the strange kinship he feels with O'Brien, and she tells him that she believes the war and Party enemies like Emmanuel Goldstein to be Party inventions. Winston is put off by her thoughtless lack of concern, and scolds her for being a rebel only from the waist down.

Summary: Chapter VI

O'Brien makes contact with Winston, who has been waiting for this moment all his life. During his brief meeting with O'Brien in the hallway at the Ministry of Truth, Winston is anxious and excited. O'Brien alludes to Syme and tells Winston that he can see a Newspeak dictionary if he will come to O'Brien's house one evening. Winston feels that his meeting with O'Brien continues a path in his life begun the day of his first rebellious thought. He thinks gloomily that this path will lead him to the Ministry of Love, where he expects to be killed. Though he accepts his fate, he is thrilled to have O'Brien's address.

Analysis: Chapters IV–VI

These three chapters represent a transitional period, during which Winston's affair with Julia becomes an established part of their lives, and leading up to Winston's meeting with O'Brien. Despite the risk, Winston rents the room above Mr. Charrington's shop so that he and Julia can have a regular place to meet. As the preparations for Hate Week cast a shadow of heat and fatigue on Winston's life, a number of important minor details surface throughout this section, each of which has some bearing on later developments in the novel.

The first to surface is the return of the glass paperweight. A "vision of the glass paperweight" inspired Winston to rent the room above the shop. The recurrence of this symbol emphasizes Winston's obsession with the past and connects it to his desire to rent the room. By making the room available for himself and Julia, he hopes he can make their relationship resemble one from an earlier, freer time. After Julia leaves the room, Winston gazes into the paperweight, imagining a world outside of time inside it, where he and Julia could float, free from the Party.

The second detail involves the prole woman singing outside the window. Winston has already thought and written in his diary that any hope for the future must come from the proles. The virile prole woman singing outside the window becomes a symbol of the hoped-for future to Winston; he imagines her bearing the children who will one day overthrow the Party.

The third factor is Winston's fear of rats. When he sees a rat in the room in Chapter IV, he shudders in terror. His worst nightmare involves rats in a vague, mysterious way he cannot quite explain. This is another foreshadow: when O'Brien tortures Winston in the Ministry of Love at the end of the novel, he will use a cage of rats to break Winston's spirit. The fact that Winston's fear of rats comes from a nightmare that he cannot explain is another important instance of the motif of dreams. Once again, Winston's dream represents an incomprehensible link to a past that is beyond his memory.

The fourth detail is the recurrence of the St. Clement's Church song. The mysterious reference the song makes continues to pique Winston's interest in the past, and its last line ("Here comes the chopper to chop off your head") continues to obliquely foreshadow his unhappy ending. A more pragmatic interest makes the song relevant in this section: Julia offers to clean the St. Clement's Church picture in Chapter IV; had she done so, the lovers would have discovered the telescreen hidden behind it.

The most important part of this section is Winston's meeting with O'Brien, which Winston considers to be the most important event of his life. The meeting is brief, but it establishes O'Brien as an enigmatic and powerful figure. At this point we cannot tell whether he is trustworthy or treacherous, whether he is truly on Winston's side or simply wants to trap him for the Party. In the end, Winston will discover the answer to that question in the place where there is no darkness.

BOOK TWO: CHAPTERS VII–VIII

SUMMARY: CHAPTER VII

One morning, Winston wakes up crying in the room above Mr. Charrington's antiques shop. Julia is with him, and asks him what is wrong. He tells her that he has been dreaming of his mother, and that until that moment, he has subconsciously believed that he murdered her. He is suddenly gripped with a sequence of memories that he had repressed. He remembers his childhood after his father left: he, his mother, and his baby sister spent most of their time in underground shelters hiding from air raids, often going without food. Consumed by hunger, Winston stole some chocolate from them and ran away, never to see them again. He hates the Party for having eliminated human feelings. He believes that the proles are still human, but that Party members like him and Julia are forced to suppress their own feelings to the point that they become virtually inhuman.

Winston and Julia worry because they know that if they are captured, they will be tortured and possibly killed, and that renting the room above Mr. Charrington's shop dramatically increases the likelihood that they *will* be captured. Fretfully, they reassure one another that although the torture will undoubtedly make them confess their crimes, it cannot make them stop loving each other. They agree that the wisest course of action would be to leave the room forever, but they cannot.

SUMMARY: CHAPTER VIII
The two take a serious risk by traveling to O'Brien's together. Inside his sumptuous apartment, O'Brien shocks Winston by turning off the telescreen. Believing that he is free of the Party's observation, Winston boldly declares that he and Julia are enemies of the Party and wish to join the Brotherhood. O'Brien tells them that the Brotherhood is real, that Emmanuel Goldstein exists and is alive, and leads them through a ritual song to initiate them into the order of rebellion. O'Brien gives them wine, and Winston proposes that they drink to the past. Julia leaves, and O'Brien promises to give Winston a copy of Goldstein's book, the manifesto of the revolution. O'Brien tells Winston that they might meet again one day. Winston asks if he means in the place where there is no darkness, and O'Brien confirms by repeating the phrase. O'Brien fills Winston in on the missing verses from the St. Clement's Church rhyme. As Winston leaves, O'Brien turns on the telescreen and returns to his work.

ANALYSIS: CHAPTERS VII–VIII
Winston's sudden surge of childhood memories reveals the depths to which the Party's psychological manipulation has infiltrated: only in his subconscious is Winston still able to cling to the truth. Julia proves to be one of the few outlets (the reader never meets any of Winston's family) for the emotionally cathartic power of this

memory, and is thus one of the few people with whom Winston can interact in a meaningful way. Their sincere commitment to each other about the fact that torture will make them turn each other in but not stop loving each other illustrates their naïve underestimation of the Party's power over the human mind. By the end of the novel, their loving words assume a kind of monstrous irony, as the only meeting between Winston and Julia following their torture proves emotionless and dull.

The most important event in this section is the meeting at O'Brien's, to which Winston is driven by a mixture of optimism and fatalism. Winston's powerful fascination with the enigmatic O'Brien leads him to trust O'Brien and feel safe in his presence, in much the same way that he feels safe in the room above Mr. Charrington's shop. Winston's hopeful belief in the Brotherhood, uncharacteristic for a man as fatalistic as he, actually contributes to his sense of impending doom. As with his first act of rebellion, he knows that his desperation to wriggle free of Party control will eventually get him caught.

O'Brien seems to represent a powerful figure willing to undermine the Party. He offers a connection to the Brotherhood, and has an iron will dedicated to fighting the Party. He knows and is interested in the past, as can be seen in his knowledge of the song about St. Clement's Church. He is the embodiment of everything Winston hoped he would be. As such, O'Brien fills Winston with a hope that he has never before experienced. Though this optimism shines brightly in the moment, it soon becomes evident that O'Brien is *acting* as Winston's ideal. The hope he inspires in Winston is part of the psychological torture Winston will soon experience, since O'Brien is simply setting Winston up for a fall.

BOOK TWO: CHAPTERS IX–X

SUMMARY: CHAPTER IX

After a ninety-hour workweek, Winston is exhausted. In the middle of Hate Week, Oceania has switched enemies and allies in the ongoing war, heaping upon Winston a tremendous amount of work to compensate for the change. At one rally, the speaker is forced to change his speech halfway through to point out that Oceania is not, and has never been, at war with Eurasia. Rather, the speaker says, Oceania is, and always has been, at war with Eastasia. The people become embarrassed about carrying the anti-Eurasia signs and blame Emmanuel Goldstein's agents for sabotaging them. Nevertheless, they exhibit full-fledged hatred for Eastasia.

In the room at Mr. Charrington's, Winston reads through Goldstein's *The Theory and Practice of Oligarchical Collectivism*, given to him by O'Brien. This lengthy book, with chapter titles taken from party slogans such as "WAR IS PEACE" and "IGNORANCE IS STRENGTH," traces a theory of social classes throughout recent history: High Class, Middle Class, and Low Class—the Inner Party, the Outer Party, and the Proles. According to the manifesto, Eurasia was created when Russia subsumed all of Europe, Oceania was created when the United States absorbed the British Empire, and Eastasia is made up of the remaining nations. These three nations keep their respective populaces preoccupied with a perpetual border war in order to preserve power among the High class. Goldstein writes that the war never advances significantly, as no two allied nations can defeat the third. The war is simply a fact of life that enables the ruling powers to keep the masses ignorant of life in other places— the real meaning of the phrase "WAR IS PEACE."

As Winston reads, Julia enters the room and flings herself into his arms. She is casually glad to know that he has the book. After half an hour in bed together, during which they hear the red-armed woman singing outside, Winston reads to Julia from the book. Goldstein explains that the control of history is a central tool of the Party. He adds that doublethink allows Inner Party members to be the most zealous about pursuing the war mentality, even though they know the falsity of the histories they write. Winston finally asks Julia if she is awake—she is not—and falls asleep himself. His last thought is that "sanity is not statistical."

SUMMARY: CHAPTER X

While Winston lies in bed the next morning, the red-armed woman outside begins to sing, waking Julia. Winston looks at the woman through the window, admires her fertility, and imagines that the proles will one day give rise to a race of conscious, independent individuals who will throw off the yoke of Party control. Winston and Julia look at the woman and realize that although they are doomed, she might hold the key to the future. Both Winston and Julia say, "We are the dead," and out of the shadows a third voice interjects, "You are the dead." Suddenly, the two realize that a telescreen is hidden behind the picture of St. Clement's Church. Stomping boots echo from outside; the house is surrounded. A familiar voice speaks the last lines of the St. Clement's rhyme: "Here comes a candle to light you to bed / Here comes a chopper to chop off your head!" The window shatters, and black-clad troops pour in. They smash the paperweight, and Winston thinks about its smallness. The troops kick Winston and beat Julia. Winston becomes disoriented; he cannot tell the time on the old-fashioned clock in the room. As the troops restrain Winston, Mr. Charrington enters the room and orders someone to pick up the shards from the shattered paperweight. Winston realizes that Mr. Charrington's voice was the one coming from the telescreen, and that Mr. Charrington is a member of the Thought Police.

ANALYSIS: CHAPTERS IX–X

The long, drawn-out excerpt from Emmanuel Goldstein's *The Theory and Practice of Oligarchical Collectivism* dominates Chapter IX, the novel's longest chapter. This sprawling treatise on political economy and class struggle mixes many sources of twentieth-century political theory, including works by Leon Trotsky and Karl Marx. Orwell combines aspects of these figures' respective political philosophies into an extended statement that some critics have felt is too long and too unwieldy to work effectively in the novel. Since *1984* is ultimately a political novel, however, some degree of political discourse seems inevitable. While Orwell may not mask this discourse very subtly or integrate it seamlessly into the rest of the novel, it suits the novel's purpose. Like titling the work *1984*, basing the Party's political philosophy on elements of contemporary political theory charges the issues of totalitarianism with striking relevance and immediacy.

Additionally, this discourse provides a long lull in the dramatic tension of the novel, setting up the surprising turn of events that the arrival of the Thought Police constitutes. The weighty political discussion coaxes the reader into a state of relaxation mirroring Winston's growing confidence in his ability to overcome the Party. Even though Winston has continually predicted his own capture throughout the novel, Orwell manages to time the arrival of the authorities perfectly to catch the reader off-guard.

The contrast between Winston and Julia is at its strongest as Winston reads to her from the manifesto in Chapter IX. Their reactions to the content succinctly reflect their personalities. While Winston finds the book to be a thrilling, joyful discovery and can hardly wait to devour it, Julia remains relatively uninterested, even falling asleep while Winston reads. Winston continues to seek an overall explanation of the Party's control over the present and the past. Julia, on the other hand, continues to seek personal pleasure in the present, not concerning herself with the larger and more abstract questions about her existence.

BOOK THREE: CHAPTERS I–III

SUMMARY: CHAPTER I

Winston sits in a bright, bare cell in which the lights are always on—he has at last arrived at the place where there is no darkness. Four telescreens monitor him. He has been transferred here from a holding cell in which a huge prole woman who shares the last name Smith wonders if she is Winston's mother. In his solitary cell, Winston envisions his captors beating him, and worries that sheer physical pain will force him to betray Julia.

Ampleforth, a poet whose crime was leaving the word "God" in a Rudyard Kipling translation, is tossed into the cell. He is soon dragged away to the dreaded Room 101, a place of mysterious and unspeakable horror. Winston shares his cell with a variety of fellow prisoners, including his flatulent neighbor Parsons, who was turned in by his own children for committing thoughtcrime.

Seeing starvation, beating, and mangling, Winston hopes dearly that the Brotherhood will send him a razorblade with which he might commit suicide. His dreams of the Brotherhood are wrecked when O'Brien, his hoped-for link to the rebellion, enters his cell. Winston cries out, "They've got you too!" To which O'Brien replies, "They got me long ago," and identifies himself as an operative of the Ministry of Love. O'Brien asserts that Winston has known O'Brien was an operative all along, and Winston admits that this is true. A guard smashes Winston's elbow, and Winston thinks that no one can become a hero in the face of physical pain because it is too much to endure.

SUMMARY: CHAPTER II

O'Brien oversees Winston's prolonged torture sessions. O'Brien tells Winston that his crime was refusing to accept the Party's control of history and his memory. As O'Brien increases the pain, Winston agrees to accept that O'Brien is holding up five fingers, though he knows that O'Brien is actually holding up only four—he agrees that anything O'Brien wants him to believe is true. He begins to love

O'Brien, because O'Brien stops the pain; he even convinces himself that O'Brien isn't the source of the pain. O'Brien tells Winston that Winston's current outlook is insane, but that torture will cure him.

> *Who controls the past controls the future. Who*
> *controls the present controls the past.*
> *(See* QUOTATIONS, *p. 43)*

O'Brien tells Winston that the Party has perfected the system practiced by the Inquisition, the Nazis, and the Soviets—it has learned how to eliminate its enemies without making martyrs of them. It converts them, and then ensures that, in the eyes of the people, they cease to exist. Slowly, Winston begins to accept O'Brien's version of events. He begins to understand how to practice doublethink, refusing to believe memories he knows are real. O'Brien offers to answer his questions, and Winston asks about Julia. O'Brien tells him that Julia betrayed him immediately. Winston asks if Big Brother exists in the same way that he himself does, and O'Brien replies that Winston does not exist. Winston asks about the Brotherhood, and O'Brien responds that Winston will never know the answer to that question. Winston asks what waits in Room 101, and O'Brien states that everyone knows what waits in Room 101.

SUMMARY: CHAPTER III

After weeks of interrogation and torture, O'Brien tells Winston about the Party's motives. Winston speculates that the Party rules the proles for their own good. O'Brien tortures him for this answer, saying that the Party's only goal is absolute, endless, and limitless power. Winston argues that the Party cannot alter the stars or the universe; O'Brien answers that it could if it needed to because the only reality that matters is in the human mind, which the Party controls.

O'Brien forces Winston to look in a mirror; he has completely deteriorated and looks gray and skeletal. Winston begins to weep and blames O'Brien for his condition. O'Brien replies that Winston knew what would happen the moment he began his diary. O'Brien acknowledges that Winston has held out by not betraying Julia, and Winston feels overwhelmed with love and gratitude toward O'Brien for recognizing his strength. However, O'Brien tells Winston not to worry, as he will soon be cured. O'Brien then notes that it doesn't matter, since, in the end, everyone is shot anyhow.

ANALYSIS: CHAPTERS I–III

Book Two saw Winston's love affair with Julia begin and end. Book Three begins his punishment and "correction." Winston's torture re-emphasizes the book's theme of the fundamental horror of physical pain—Winston cannot stop the torture or prevent the psychological control O'Brien gains from torturing him, and when the guard smashes his elbow, he thinks that nothing in the world is worse than physical pain. Though the Party's ability to manipulate the minds of its subjects is the key to the breadth of its power, its ability to control their bodies is what makes it finally impossible to resist.

Up to this point, O'Brien has remained an enigma to the reader, but his arrival toward the beginning of Winston's prison term places him firmly on the side of the Party. O'Brien seems to have been a rebel like Winston at one point—when Winston asks if he too has been taken prisoner, O'Brien replies, "They got me a long time ago." O'Brien adds insult to Winston's imprisonment by claiming that Winston knew all along that he was affiliated with the Party—and Winston knows he is right. This section seems to imply that Winston's fatalism stems as much from his understanding of his own fatalistic motives as from his belief in the power of the Party. In other words, Winston's belief that he would ultimately be caught no matter what he did enabled him to convince himself to trust O'Brien. He knew that he would be caught whether he trusted O'Brien or not, and so he let himself trust O'Brien simply because he deeply wanted to do so.

Winston's obsession with O'Brien, which began with the dream about the place where there is no darkness, was the source of his undoing, and it undoes him now as well. Orwell explores the theme of how physical pain affects the human mind, and arrives at the conclusion that it grants extraordinary emotional power to the person capable of inflicting the pain. Because O'Brien tortures him, Winston perversely comes to love O'Brien. Throughout the torture sessions, Winston becomes increasingly eager to believe anything O'Brien tells him—even Party slogans and rhetoric. In the next section of the novel, Winston even begins to dream about O'Brien in the same way that he now dreams about his mother and Julia.

BOOK THREE: CHAPTERS IV–VI

SUMMARY: CHAPTER IV

After some time, Winston is transferred to a more comfortable room and the torture eases. He dreams contently of Julia, his mother, and O'Brien in the Golden Country. He gains weight and is allowed to write on a small slate. He comes to the conclusion that he was foolish to oppose the Party alone, and tries to make himself believe in Party slogans. He writes on his slate "FREEDOM IS SLAVERY," "TWO AND TWO MAKE FIVE," and "GOD IS POWER."

One day, in a sudden, passionate fit of misery, Winston screams out Julia's name many times, terrifying himself. Though he knows that crying out in this way will lead O'Brien to torture him, he realizes his deep desire to continue hating the Party. He tries to bottle up his hatred so that even he will not recognize it. Therefore, when the Party kills him, he will die hating Big Brother—a personal victory. But he cannot hide his feelings. When O'Brien arrives with the guards, Winston tells him that he hates Big Brother. O'Brien replies that obeying Big Brother is not sufficient—Winston must learn to love him. O'Brien then instructs the guards to take Winston to Room 101.

SUMMARY: CHAPTER V

In Room 101, O'Brien straps Winston to a chair, then clamps Winston's head so that he cannot move. He tells Winston that Room 101 contains "the worst thing in the world." He reminds Winston of his worst nightmare—the dream of being in a dark place with something terrible on the other side of the wall—and informs him that rats are on the other side of the wall. O'Brien picks up a cage full of enormous, squirming rats and places it near Winston. He says that when he presses a lever, the door will slide up and the rats will leap onto Winston's face and eat it. With the writhing, starving rats just inches away, Winston cracks. He screams that he wants O'Brien to subject Julia to this torture instead of him. O'Brien, satisfied by this betrayal, removes the cage.

SUMMARY: CHAPTER VI

Winston, now free, sits at the Chestnut Tree Café, where dismissed Party members go to drink. He enjoys a glass of Victory Gin and watches the telescreen. He accepts everything the Party says and does. Without acknowledging it to himself, he can still smell the rats. On the table, Winston traces "2 + 2 = 5" in the dust. He remembers seeing Julia on a bitter-cold day that March. She had thickened and stiffened, and he now found the thought of sex with her repulsive. They acknowledged that they had betrayed one another, and agreed to meet again, though neither is truly interested in continuing their relationship. Winston thinks he hears the song lyrics "Under the spreading chestnut tree / I sold you and you sold me," which he heard when he saw the political prisoners there many years earlier. He begins to cry. He remembers a moment of happiness with his mother and sister, but thinks it must be a false memory. He looks up and sees a picture of Big Brother on the telescreen, making him feel happy and safe. As he listens to the war news, he reassures himself of both the great victory he has won over himself and his newfound love for Big Brother.

> *And perhaps you might pretend, afterwards, that it was only a trick and that you just said it to make them stop and didn't really mean it. But that isn't true.*
> *(See* QUOTATIONS, *p. 45)*

SUMMARY & ANALYSIS

ANALYSIS: CHAPTERS IV–VI

Though his stay at the Ministry of Love has broken his mind and will and though his love for Big Brother precludes the need to think for himself, Winston still envisions the day that the Party will shoot him. This apparent death wish has led to some speculation that the key to Winston's character is his fatalism, that he rebels against the Party not because he desires freedom, but because he wants the Party to kill him. Given Orwell's political aspirations for *1984*, this consideration seems to diminish the intent of the work. *1984* may include psychological imbalance among its list of ill effects of totalitarian government, but it seems clear that it is not primarily about psychological imbalance. The main purpose of the novel is to chronicle the workings of the Party's control over the minds of its subjects in order to warn readers of the dangers of totalitarianism. If all of Winston's problems were caused by an innate, unusual psychological disorder, then this overriding theme would become irrelevant.

Many consider *1984*'s pivotal scene—in which O'Brien threatens to release the cage of rats on Winston's face—an anticlimax. It has been argued that the cage of rats is not horrible enough to make the reader feel Winston's torment, and that it is an arbitrary device, unrelated to the powerful, sophisticated workings of the Party. At first glance, these criticisms seem valid. Winston's collapse does follow hard upon his passionate restatement of his love for Julia and hatred for Big Brother in Chapter IV. However, it is important to remember the theme of physical control, which manifests itself in the Party's manipulation of the body: Orwell consistently argues that physical pain and the sense of physical danger can override human reason. Winston, facing a writhing swarm of rats prepared to devour his face, cannot act rationally. That his betrayal of Julia occurs so soon after he restates his love for her is precisely the point, as physical pain eliminates the possibility of defending emotional conviction. As Winston notes earlier in the novel, he is a prisoner of his own nervous system. Turning against Julia is an instinctive lunge for self-preservation. Rather than the rats themselves, it is the awareness, foisted upon him by the Party, that he is a prisoner of his own body that ultimately breaks Winston. Once he believes that he is limited by his body, he has no reason to think, act, or rebel.

APPENDIX: THE PRINCIPLES OF NEWSPEAK

The Appendix of *1984* stands as Orwell's explanation of Newspeak, the official language of Oceania. Although Orwell felt that these ideas were too technical to completely integrate into the novel, they support the novel's stance on language and thought in relation to the public's acceptance of governmental control.

Newspeak is the official language of Oceania, scheduled for official adoption around 2050, and designed to make the ideological premises of Ingsoc (Newspeak for English Socialism, the Party's official political alignment) the only expressible doctrine. Newspeak is engineered to remove even the *possibility* of rebellious thoughts—the words by which such thoughts might be articulated have been eliminated from the language. Newspeak contains no negative terms. For example, the only way to express the meaning of "bad" is through the word "ungood." Something extremely bad is called "doubleplus ungood."

Newspeak's grammar is arranged so that any word can serve as any part of speech, and there are three different groups of vocabulary words. The A vocabulary contains everyday words and phrases, as Orwell says, "for such things as eating, drinking, working" and so on. In comparison with modern English, these words are fewer in number but more rigid in meaning. Newspeak leaves no room for nuance, or for degrees of meaning. The B vocabulary of Newspeak contains all words with political or ideological significance, specially tailored to engender blind acceptance of the Party's doctrines. For example, "goodthink" means roughly the same thing as "orthodoxy." The B vocabulary consists entirely of compound words and often compresses words into smaller forms to achieve conceptual simplicity: the English phrase "Thought Police," for instance, is compressed into "thinkpol"; "the Ministry of Love" becomes "miniluv." The C vocabulary encompasses words that relate specifically to science and to technical fields and disciplines. It is designed to ensure that technical knowledge remains segmented among many fields, so that no one individual can gain access to too much knowledge. In fact, there is no word for "science"; as Orwell writes, "*Ingsoc*" covers any meaning that such a concept could possibly have.

The particularities of Newspeak make it impossible to translate most older English (oldspeak) texts into the language; the introduction of the Declaration of Independence, for instance, can be translated only into a single word: crimethink. Furthermore, a great many technical manuals must be translated into Newspeak; it is this bulk of translation work that explains the Party's decision to postpone the full adoption of Newspeak to 2050.

Important Quotations
Explained

1. WAR IS PEACE
    FREEDOM IS SLAVERY
    IGNORANCE IS STRENGTH

These words are the official slogans of the Party, and are inscribed in massive letters on the white pyramid of the Ministry of Truth, as Winston observes in Book One, Chapter I. Because it is introduced so early in the novel, this creed serves as the reader's first introduction to the idea of doublethink. By weakening the independence and strength of individuals' minds and forcing them to live in a constant state of propaganda-induced fear, the Party is able to force its subjects to accept anything it decrees, even if it is entirely illogical—for instance, the Ministry of Peace is in charge of waging war, the Ministry of Love is in charge of political torture, and the Ministry of Truth is in charge of doctoring history books to reflect the Party's ideology.

That the national slogan of Oceania is equally contradictory is an important testament to the power of the Party's mass campaign of psychological control. In theory, the Party is able to maintain that "War Is Peace" because having a common enemy keeps the people of Oceania united. "Freedom Is Slavery" because, according to the Party, the man who is independent is doomed to fail. By the same token, "Slavery Is Freedom," because the man subjected to the collective will is free from danger and want. "Ignorance Is Strength" because the inability of the people to recognize these contradictions cements the power of the authoritarian regime.

2. Who controls the past controls the future. Who controls
    the present controls the past.

This Party slogan appears twice in the novel, once in Book One, Chapter III, when Winston is thinking about the Party's control of history and memory, and once in Book Three, Chapter II, when Winston, now a prisoner in the Ministry of Love, talks to O'Brien about the nature of the past. The slogan is an important example of the Party's technique of using false history to break down the psychological independence of its subjects. Control of the past ensures control of the future, because the past can be treated essentially as a set of conditions that justify or encourage future goals: if the past was idyllic, then people will act to re-create it; if the past was nightmarish, then people will act to prevent such circumstances from recurring. The Party creates a past that was a time of misery and slavery from which it claims to have liberated the human race, thus compelling people to work toward the Party's goals.

The Party has complete political power in the present, enabling it to control the way in which its subjects think about and interpret the past: every history book reflects Party ideology, and individuals are forbidden from keeping mementos of their own pasts, such as photographs and documents. As a result, the citizens of Oceania have a very short, fuzzy memory, and are willing to believe anything that the Party tells them. In the second appearance of this quote, O'Brien tells Winston that the past has no concrete existence and that it is real only in the minds of human beings. O'Brien is essentially arguing that because the Party's version of the past is what people believe, that past, though it has no basis in real events, has become the truth.

QUOTATIONS

3.   In the end the Party would announce that two and two made five, and you would have to believe it. It was inevitable that they should make that claim sooner or later: the logic of their position demanded it. Not merely the validity of experience, but the very existence of external reality was tacitly denied by their philosophy.

This quote occurs in Book One, Chapter VII, as Winston looks at a children's history book and marvels at the Party's control of the human mind. These lines play into the theme of psychological manipulation. In this case, Winston considers the Party's exploitation of its fearful subjects as a means to suppress the intellectual notion of objective reality. If the universe exists only in the mind, and the Party controls the mind, then the Party controls the universe. As Winston thinks, "For, after all, how do we know that two and two make four? Or that the force of gravity works? Or that the past is unchangeable? If both the past and the external world exist only in the mind, and if the mind itself is controllable—what then?" The mathematical sentence 2 + 2 = 5 thus becomes a motif linked to the theme of psychological independence. Early in the novel, Winston writes that "Freedom is the freedom to say that two plus two make four." The motif comes full circle at the end of the novel after the torture Winston suffers in the Ministry of Love breaks his soul; he sits at the Chestnut Tree Café and traces "2 + 2 = 5" in the dust on his table.

4. And when memory failed and written records were falsified—when that happened, the claim of the Party to have improved the conditions of human life had got to be accepted, because there did not exist, and never again could exist, any standard against which it could be tested.

This quote from Book One, Chapter VIII, emphasizes how one's understanding of the past affects one's attitude about the present. Winston has just had a frustrating conversation with an old man about life before the Revolution, and he realizes that the Party has deliberately set out to weaken people's memories in order to render them unable to challenge what the Party claims about the present. If no one remembers life before the Revolution, then no one can say that the Party has failed mankind by forcing people to live in conditions of poverty, filth, ignorance, and hunger. Rather, the Party uses rewritten history books and falsified records to prove its good deeds.

5. And perhaps you might pretend, afterwards, that it was only a trick and that you just said it to make them stop and didn't really mean it. But that isn't true. At the time when it happens you do mean it. You think there's no other way of saving yourself and you're quite ready to save yourself that way. You want it to happen to the other person. You don't give a damn what they suffer. All you care about is yourself.

Julia speaks these lines to Winston in Book Three, Chapter VI, as they discuss what happened to them in Room 101. She tells him that she wanted her torture to be shifted to him, and he responds that he felt exactly the same way. These acts of mutual betrayal represent the Party's final psychological victory. Soon after their respective experiences in Room 101, Winston and Julia are set free as they no longer pose a threat to the Party. Here, Julia says that despite her efforts to make herself feel better, she knows that in order to save herself she really did want the Party to torture Winston. In the end, the Party proves to Winston and Julia that no moral conviction or emotional loyalty is strong enough to withstand torture. Physical pain and fear will always cause people to betray their convictions if doing so will end their suffering.

Winston comes to a similar conclusion during his own stint at the Ministry of Love, bringing to its culmination the novel's theme of physical control: control over the body ultimately grants the Party control over the mind. As with most of the Party's techniques, there is an extremely ironic strain of doublethink running underneath: self-love and self-preservation, the underlying components of individualism and independence, lead one to fear pain and suffering, ultimately causing one to accept the principles of anti-individualist collectivism that allows the Party to thrive.

Key Facts

FULL TITLE
1984

AUTHOR
George Orwell

TYPE OF WORK
Novel

GENRE
Negative utopian, or dystopian, fiction

LANGUAGE
English

TIME AND PLACE WRITTEN
England, 1949

DATE OF FIRST PUBLICATION
1949

PUBLISHER
Harcourt Brace Jovanovich, Inc.

NARRATOR
Third-person, limited

CLIMAX
Winston's torture with the cage of rats in Room 101

PROTAGONIST
Winston Smith

ANTAGONIST
The Party; Big Brother

SETTING (TIME)
1984

SETTING (PLACE)
London, England (known as "Airstrip One" in the novel's alternate reality)

POINT OF VIEW

Winston Smith's

FALLING ACTION

Winston's time in the café following his release from prison, including the memory of his meeting with Julia at the end of Book Three

TENSE

Past

FORESHADOWING

Winston's dreams (making love to Julia in the forest, meeting O'Brien in the "place where there is no darkness"); the St. Clement's Church song ("Here comes a chopper to chop off your head!")

TONE

Dark, frustrated, pessimistic

THEMES

The psychological, technological, physical, and social dangers of totalitarianism and political authority; the importance of language in shaping human thought

MOTIFS

Urban decay (London is falling apart under the Party's leadership); the idea of doublethink (the ability to hold two contradictory ideas in one's mind at the same time and believe them both to be true)

SYMBOLS

The glass paperweight (Winston's desire to connect with the past); the red-armed prole woman (the hope that the proles will ultimately rise up against the Party); the picture of St. Clement's Church (the past); the telescreens and the posters of Big Brother (the Party's constant surveillance of its subjects); the phrase "the place where there is no darkness" (Winston's tendency to mask his fatalism with false hope, as the place where there is no darkness turns out to be not a paradise but a prison cell)

Study Questions

1.   *1984 is full of images and ideas that do not directly affect the plot, but nevertheless attain thematic importance. What are some of these symbols and motifs, and how does Orwell use them?*

Some of the most important symbols and motifs in 1984 include Winston's paperweight, the St. Clement's Church picture and the rhyme associated with it, the prole woman singing outside the window, and the phrase "the place where there is no darkness." In addition to unifying the novel, these symbols and motifs represent Winston's attempts to escape or undermine the oppressive rule of the Party. Winston conceives of the singing prole woman as an incubator for future rebels; she symbolizes for him the eventual overthrow of the Party by the working class. The St. Clement's Church picture is a double symbol. For Winston it symbolizes a stolen past, but it also symbolizes the Party's complete power and betrayal of humanity, since the picture hides the telescreen by which the Party monitors Winston when he believes himself to be safe. The St. Clement's song is a mysterious, ominous, and enigmatic relic of the past for Winston and Julia. Its ending—"Here comes the chopper to chop off your head!"—foreshadows their eventual capture and torture.

Winston's paperweight is another symbol of the past, but it also comes to represent a kind of temporal stasis in which Winston can dream without fear, imagining himself floating inside the glass walls of the paperweight with his mother. The phrase "the place where there is no darkness" works as another symbol of escapist hope throughout the novel, as Winston recalls the dream in which O'Brien tells him about this place and says that they will meet there one day. The phrase therefore orients Winston toward the end of the novel, when the phrase becomes bitterly ironic: the place where there is no darkness is the Ministry of Love, where the lights remain on in the prisons all day and all night.

2. *Discuss the idea of doublethink. How important is doublethink to the Party's control of Oceania? How important is it to Winston's brainwashing?*

One of the most compelling aspects of 1984 is Orwell's understanding of the roles that thought and language play in rebellion and control. In Newspeak, Orwell invents a language that will make rebellion impossible, because the words to conceive of such an action cease to exist. Doublethink, the ability to maintain two contradictory ideas in one's head simultaneously and believe them both to be true, functions as a psychological mechanism that explains people's willingness to accept control over their memories and their past. Doublethink is crucial to the Party's control of Oceania, because it enables the Party to alter historical records and pass off these distorted accounts as authentic. The brainwashed populace no longer recognizes contradictions. Instead, it accepts the Party's version of the past as accurate, even though that representation may change from minute to minute.

Emmanuel Goldstein's manifesto even suggests that doublethink is strongest among the powerful Inner Party members who convince themselves that they act for Big Brother, even though they know that Big Brother is a myth. Doublethink is equally crucial to Winston's gradual conversion to loving Big Brother because it enables him to accept his torturers' words as true, even though his own fading memories—of the photograph of the three Party traitors, for instance—contradict them.

3. *Describe Julia's character as it relates to Winston. How is she different from him? How is she similar to him? How does Julia's age make her attitude toward the Party very different from Winston's?*

Winston is thirty-nine, and Julia is twenty-six. His childhood took place largely before the Party came to power around 1960 (as he remembers it). Julia, on the other hand, is a child of the Party era. Many of the regime's elements that seem most frightening and evil to Winston fail to upset or even faze Julia. Like Winston, she hates the Party and sees through many of its techniques. She understands, for instance, that it uses sexual repression to control the populace. She even has a better intuitive grasp of the Party's methods than Winston does, planning their affair and often explaining aspects of the Party to him. However, the Party's large-scale control of history does not interest or trouble her as it does Winston, because she does not remember a time when the Party was not in control.

In stark defiance of Party doctrine, Julia enjoys sex and rebels against the Party in small ways. But growing up under the Party regime has made her apathetic to the difference between truth and falsehood. She has no patience for Winston's desire for a categorical, abstract rejection of Party doctrine. Rather, she falls asleep when Winston reads to her from Emmanuel Goldstein's book, epitomizing her simple, self-centered, pleasure-seeking approach to life.

STUDY QUESTIONS

How to Write
Literary Analysis

The Literary Essay: A Step-by-Step Guide

When you read for pleasure, your only goal is enjoyment. You might find yourself reading to get caught up in an exciting story, to learn about an interesting time or place, or just to pass time. Maybe you're looking for inspiration, guidance, or a reflection of your own life. There are as many different, valid ways of reading a book as there are books in the world.

When you read a work of literature in an English class, however, you're being asked to read in a special way: you're being asked to perform *literary analysis*. To analyze something means to break it down into smaller parts and then examine how those parts work, both individually and together. Literary analysis involves examining all the parts of a novel, play, short story, or poem—elements such as character, setting, tone, and imagery—and thinking about how the author uses those elements to create certain effects.

A literary essay isn't a book review: you're not being asked whether or not you liked a book or not or whether you'd recommend it to another reader. A literary essay also isn't like the kind of book report you wrote when you were younger, where your teacher wanted you to summarize the book's action. A high school- or college-level literary essay asks, "How does this piece of literature actually work?" "How does it do what it does?" and, "Why might the author have made the choices he or she did?"

The Seven Steps

No one is born knowing how to analyze literature; it's a skill you learn and a process you can master. As you gain more practice with this kind of thinking and writing, you'll be able to craft a method that works best for you. But until then, here are seven basic steps to writing a well-constructed literary essay:

1. *Ask questions*
2. *Collect evidence*
3. *Construct a thesis*

4. Develop and organize arguments
5. Write the introduction
6. Write the body paragraphs
7. Write the conclusion

_____

1. Ask Questions

When you're assigned a literary essay in class, your teacher will often provide you with a list of writing prompts. Lucky you! Now all you have to do is choose one. Do yourself a favor and pick a topic that interests you. You'll have a much better (not to mention easier) time if you start off with something you enjoy thinking about. If you are asked to come up with a topic by yourself, though, you might start to feel a little panicked. Maybe you have too many ideas—or none at all. Don't worry. Take a deep breath and start by asking yourself these questions:

- **What struck you?** Did a particular image, line, or scene linger in your mind for a long time? If it fascinated you, chances are you can draw on it to write a fascinating essay.

- **What confused you?** Maybe you were surprised to see a character act in a certain way, or maybe you didn't understand why the book ended the way it did. Confusing moments in a work of literature are like a loose thread in a sweater: if you pull on it, you can unravel the entire thing. Ask yourself why the author chose to write about that character or scene the way he or she did and you might tap into some important insights about the work as a whole.

- **Did you notice any patterns?** Is there a phrase that the main character uses constantly or an image that repeats throughout the book? If you can figure out how that pattern weaves through the work and what the significance of that pattern is, you've almost got your entire essay mapped out.

- **Did you notice any contradictions or ironies?** Great works of literature are complex; great literary essays recognize and explain those complexities. Maybe the title (*Happy Days*) totally disagrees with the book's subject matter (hungry orphans dying in the woods). Maybe the main character acts one way around his family and a completely different way around his friends and associates. If you can find a way to explain a work's contradictory elements, you've got the seeds of a great essay.

At this point, you don't need to know exactly what you're going to say about your topic; you just need a place to begin your exploration. You can help direct your reading and brainstorming by formulating your topic as a *question,* which you'll then try to answer in your essay. The best questions invite critical debates and discussions, not just a rehashing of the summary. Remember, you're looking for something you can *prove or argue* based on evidence you find in the text. Finally, remember to keep the scope of your question in mind: is this a topic you can adequately address within the word or page limit you've been given? Conversely, is this a topic big enough to fill the required length?

GOOD QUESTIONS

"Are Romeo and Juliet's parents responsible for the deaths of their children?"

"Why do pigs keep showing up in LORD OF THE FLIES?*"*

"Are Dr. Frankenstein and his monster alike? How?"

BAD QUESTIONS

"What happens to Scout in TO KILL A MOCKINGBIRD?*"*

"What do the other characters in JULIUS CAESAR *think about Caesar?"*

"How does Hester Prynne in THE SCARLET LETTER *remind me of my sister?"*

2. COLLECT EVIDENCE

Once you know what question you want to answer, it's time to scour the book for things that will help you answer the question. Don't worry if you don't know what you want to say yet—right now you're just collecting ideas and material and letting it all percolate. Keep track of passages, symbols, images, or scenes that deal with your topic. Eventually, you'll start making connections between these examples and your thesis will emerge.

Here's a brief summary of the various parts that compose each and every work of literature. These are the elements that you will analyze in your essay, and which you will offer as evidence to support your arguments. For more on the parts of literary works, see the Glossary of Literary Terms at the end of this section.

ELEMENTS OF STORY   These are the *what*s of the work—what happens, where it happens, and to whom it happens.

- **Plot:** All of the events and actions of the work.
- **Character:** The people who act and are acted upon in a literary work. The main character of a work is known as the *protagonist*.
- **Conflict:** The central tension in the work. In most cases, the protagonist wants something, while opposing forces (antagonists) hinder the protagonist's progress.
- **Setting:** When and where the work takes place. Elements of setting include location, time period, time of day, weather, social atmosphere, and economic conditions.
- **Narrator:** The person telling the story. The narrator may straightforwardly report what happens, convey the subjective opinions and perceptions of one or more characters, or provide commentary and opinion in his or her own voice.
- **Themes:** The main idea or message of the work—usually an abstract idea about people, society, or life in general. A work may have many themes, which may be in tension with one another.

ELEMENTS OF STYLE   These are the *how*s—how the characters speak, how the story is constructed, and how language is used throughout the work.

- **Structure and organization:** How the parts of the work are assembled. Some novels are narrated in a linear, chronological fashion, while others skip around in time. Some plays follow a traditional three- or five-act structure, while others are a series of loosely connected scenes. Some authors deliberately leave gaps in their works, leaving readers to puzzle out the missing information. A work's structure and organization can tell you a lot about the kind of message it wants to convey.
- **Point of view:** The perspective from which a story is told. In *first-person point of view*, the narrator involves him or herself in the story. ("I went to the store"; "We watched in horror as the bird slammed into the window.") A first-person narrator is usually the protagonist of the work, but not always. In *third-person point of view*, the narrator does not participate

in the story. A third-person narrator may closely follow a specific character, recounting that individual character's thoughts or experiences, or it may be what we call an *omniscient* narrator. Omniscient narrators see and know all: they can witness any event in any time or place and are privy to the inner thoughts and feelings of all characters. Remember that the narrator and the author are not the same thing!

- **Diction:** Word choice. Whether a character uses dry, clinical language or flowery prose with lots of exclamation points can tell you a lot about his or her attitude and personality.

- **Syntax:** Word order and sentence construction. Syntax is a crucial part of establishing an author's narrative voice. Ernest Hemingway, for example, is known for writing in very short, straightforward sentences, while James Joyce characteristically wrote in long, incredibly complicated lines.

- **Tone:** The mood or feeling of the text. Diction and syntax often contribute to the tone of a work. A novel written in short, clipped sentences that use small, simple words might feel brusque, cold, or matter-of-fact.

- **Imagery:** Language that appeals to the senses, representing things that can be seen, smelled, heard, tasted, or touched.

- **Figurative language:** Language that is not meant to be interpreted literally. The most common types of figurative language are *metaphors* and *similes,* which compare two unlike things in order to suggest a similarity between them— for example, "All the world's a stage," or "The moon is like a ball of green cheese." (Metaphors say one thing *is* another thing; similes claim that one thing is *like* another thing.)

---

3. CONSTRUCT A THESIS

When you've examined all the evidence you've collected and know how you want to answer the question, it's time to write your thesis statement. A *thesis* is a claim about a work of literature that needs to be supported by evidence and arguments. The thesis statement is the heart of the literary essay, and the bulk of your paper will be spent trying to prove this claim. A good thesis will be:

- **Arguable**. "*The Great Gatsby* describes New York society in the 1920s" isn't a thesis—it's a fact.

- **Provable through textual evidence**. "*Hamlet* is a confusing but ultimately very well-written play" is a weak thesis because it offers the writer's personal opinion about the book. Yes, it's arguable, but it's not a claim that can be proved or supported with examples taken from the play itself.

- **Surprising**. "Both George and Lenny change a great deal in *Of Mice and Men*" is a weak thesis because it's obvious. A really strong thesis will argue for a reading of the text that is not immediately apparent.

- **Specific.** "Dr. Frankenstein's monster tells us a lot about the human condition" is *almost* a really great thesis statement, but it's still too vague. What does the writer mean by "a lot"? *How* does the monster tell us so much about the human condition?

GOOD THESIS STATEMENTS

Question: In *Romeo and Juliet*, which is more powerful in shaping the lovers' story: fate or foolishness?

Thesis: "Though Shakespeare defines Romeo and Juliet as 'star-crossed lovers' and images of stars and planets appear throughout the play, a closer examination of that celestial imagery reveals that the stars are merely witnesses to the characters' foolish activities and not the causes themselves."

Question: How does the bell jar function as a symbol in Sylvia Plath's *The Bell Jar*?

Thesis: "A bell jar is a bell-shaped glass that has three basic uses: to hold a specimen for observation, to contain gases, and to maintain a vacuum. The bell jar appears in each of these capacities in *The Bell Jar*, Plath's semi-autobiographical novel, and each appearances marks a different stage in Esther's mental breakdown."

Question: Would Piggy in *The Lord of the Flies* make a good island leader if he were given the chance?

Thesis: "Though the intelligent, rational, and innovative Piggy has the mental characteristics of a good leader, he ultimately lacks the social skills necessary to be an effective one. Golding emphasizes this point by giving Piggy a foil in the charismatic Jack, whose magnetic personality allows him to capture and wield power effectively, if not always wisely."

LITERARY ANALYSIS

4. DEVELOP AND ORGANIZE ARGUMENTS

The reasons and examples that support your thesis will form the middle paragraphs of your essay. Since you can't really write your thesis statement until you know how you'll structure your argument, you'll probably end up working on steps 3 and 4 at the same time.

There's no single method of argumentation that will work in every context. One essay prompt might ask you to compare and contrast two characters, while another asks you to trace an image through a given work of literature. These questions require different kinds of answers and therefore different kinds of arguments. Below, we'll discuss three common kinds of essay prompts and some strategies for constructing a solid, well-argued case.

TYPES OF LITERARY ESSAYS

- **Compare and contrast**

  Compare and contrast the characters of Huck and Jim in THE ADVENTURES OF HUCKLEBERRY FINN.

  Chances are you've written this kind of essay before. In an academic literary context, you'll organize your arguments the same way you would in any other class. You can either go *subject by subject* or *point by point*. In the former, you'll discuss one character first and then the second. In the latter, you'll choose several traits (attitude toward life, social status, images and metaphors associated with the character) and devote a paragraph to each. You may want to use a mix of these two approaches—for example, you may want to spend a paragraph a piece broadly sketching Huck's and Jim's personalities before transitioning into a paragraph or two that describes a few key points of comparison. This can be a highly effective strategy if you want to make a counterintuitive argument—that, despite seeming to be totally different, the two objects being compared are actually similar in a very important way (or vice versa). Remember that your essay should reveal something fresh or unexpected about the text, so think beyond the obvious parallels and differences.

- **Trace**

  Choose an image—for example, birds, knives, or eyes—and trace that image throughout MACBETH.

  Sounds pretty easy, right? All you need to do is read the play, underline every appearance of a knife in *Macbeth,* and then list them in your essay in the order they appear, right? Well, not exactly. Your teacher doesn't want a simple catalog of examples. He or she wants to see you make *connections* between those examples—that's the difference between summarizing and analyzing. In the *Macbeth* example above, think about the different contexts in which knives appear in the play and to what effect. In *Macbeth*, there are real knives and imagined knives; knives that kill and knives that simply threaten. Categorize and classify your examples to give them some order. Finally, always keep the overall effect in mind. After you choose and analyze your examples, you should come to some greater understanding about the work, as well as your chosen image, symbol, or phrase's role in developing the major themes and stylistic strategies of that work.

- **Debate**

   Is the society depicted in 1984 *good for its citizens?*

   In this kind of essay, you're being asked to debate a moral, ethical, or aesthetic issue regarding the work. You might be asked to judge a character or group of characters (*Is Caesar responsible for his own demise?*) or the work itself (*Is* JANE EYRE *a feminist novel?*). For this kind of essay, there are two important points to keep in mind. First, don't simply base your arguments on your personal feelings and reactions. Every literary essay expects you to read and analyze the work, so search for evidence in the text. What do characters in *1984* have to say about the government of Oceania? What images does Orwell use that might give you a hint about his attitude toward the government? As in any debate, you also need to make sure that you define all the necessary terms before you begin to argue your case. What does it mean to be a "good" society? What makes a novel "feminist"? You should define your terms right up front, in the first paragraph after your introduction.

   Second, remember that strong literary essays make contrary and surprising arguments. Try to think outside the box. In the *1984* example above, it seems like the obvious answer would be no, the totalitarian society depicted in Orwell's novel is *not* good for its citizens. But can you think of any arguments for the opposite side? Even if your final assertion is that the novel depicts a cruel, repressive, and therefore harmful society, acknowledging and responding to the counterargument will strengthen your overall case.

LITERARY ANALYSIS

5. WRITE THE INTRODUCTION

Your introduction sets up the entire essay. It's where you present your topic and articulate the particular issues and questions you'll be addressing. It's also where you, as the writer, introduce yourself to your readers. A persuasive literary essay immediately establishes its writer as a knowledgeable, authoritative figure.

An introduction can vary in length depending on the overall length of the essay, but in a traditional five-paragraph essay it should be no longer than one paragraph. However long it is, your introduction needs to:

- **Provide any necessary context.** Your introduction should situate the reader and let him or her know what to expect. What book are you discussing? Which characters? What topic will you be addressing?

- **Answer the "So what?" question.** Why is this topic important, and why is your particular position on the topic noteworthy? Ideally, your introduction should pique the reader's interest by suggesting how your argument is surprising or otherwise counterintuitive. Literary essays make unexpected connections and reveal less-than-obvious truths.

- **Present your thesis.** This usually happens at or very near the end of your introduction.

- **Indicate the shape of the essay to come.** Your reader should finish reading your introduction with a good sense of the scope of your essay as well as the path you'll take toward proving your thesis. You don't need to spell out every step, but you do need to suggest the organizational pattern you'll be using.

Your introduction should not:

- **Be vague.** Beware of the two killer words in literary analysis: *interesting* and *important*. Of course the work, question, or example is interesting and important—that's why you're writing about it!

- **Open with any grandiose assertions.** Many student readers think that beginning their essays with a flamboyant statement such as, "Since the dawn of time, writers have been fascinated with the topic of free will," makes them sound important and commanding. You know what? It actually sounds pretty amateurish.

- **Wildly praise the work.** Another typical mistake student writers make is extolling the work or author. Your teacher doesn't need to be told that "Shakespeare is perhaps the greatest writer in the English language." You can mention a work's reputation in passing—by referring to *The Adventures of Huckleberry Finn* as "Mark Twain's enduring classic," for example—but don't make a point of bringing it up unless that reputation is key to your argument.

- **Go off-topic.** Keep your introduction streamlined and to the point. Don't feel the need to throw in all kinds of bells and whistles in order to impress your reader—just get to the point as quickly as you can, without skimping on any of the required steps.

---

6. WRITE THE BODY PARAGRAPHS

Once you've written your introduction, you'll take the arguments you developed in step 4 and turn them into your body paragraphs. The organization of this middle section of your essay will largely be determined by the argumentative strategy you use, but no matter how you arrange your thoughts, your body paragraphs need to do the following:

- **Begin with a strong topic sentence.** Topic sentences are like signs on a highway: they tell the reader where they are and where they're going. A good topic sentence not only alerts readers to what issue will be discussed in the following paragraph but also gives them a sense of what argument will be made *about* that issue. "Rumor and gossip play an important role in *The Crucible*" isn't a strong topic sentence because it doesn't tell us very much. "The community's constant gossiping creates an environment that allows false accusations to flourish" is a much stronger topic sentence— it not only tells us *what* the paragraph will discuss (gossip) but *how* the paragraph will discuss the topic (by showing how gossip creates a set of conditions that leads to the play's climactic action).

- **Fully and completely develop a single thought.** Don't skip around in your paragraph or try to stuff in too much material. Body paragraphs are like bricks: each individual one needs to be strong and sturdy or the entire structure will collapse. Make sure you have really proven your point before moving on to the next one.

- **Use transitions effectively.** Good literary essay writers know that each paragraph must be clearly and strongly linked to the material around it. Think of each paragraph as a response to the one that precedes it. Use transition words and phrases such as *however, similarly, on the contrary, therefore*, and *furthermore* to indicate what kind of response you're making.

---

7. WRITE THE CONCLUSION

Just as you used the introduction to ground your readers in the topic before providing your thesis, you'll use the conclusion to quickly summarize the specifics learned thus far and then hint at the broader implications of your topic. A good conclusion will:

- **Do more than simply restate the thesis.** If your thesis argued that *The Catcher in the Rye* can be read as a Christian allegory, don't simply end your essay by saying, "And that is why *The Catcher in the Rye* can be read as a Christian allegory." If you've constructed your arguments well, this kind of statement will just be redundant.

- **Synthesize the arguments, not summarize them.** Similarly, don't repeat the details of your body paragraphs in your conclusion. The reader has already read your essay, and chances are it's not so long that they've forgotten all your points by now.

- **Revisit the "So what?" question.** In your introduction, you made a case for why your topic and position are important. You should close your essay with the same sort of gesture. What do your readers know now that they didn't know before? How will that knowledge help them better appreciate or understand the work overall?

- **Move from the specific to the general.** Your essay has most likely treated a very specific element of the work—a single character, a small set of images, or a particular passage. In your conclusion, try to show how this narrow discussion has wider implications for the work overall. If your essay on *To Kill a Mockingbird* focused on the character of Boo Radley, for example, you might want to include a bit in your conclusion about how he fits into the novel's larger message about childhood, innocence, or family life.

- **Stay relevant.** Your conclusion should suggest new directions of thought, but it shouldn't be treated as an opportunity to pad your essay with all the extra, interesting ideas you came up with during your brainstorming sessions but couldn't fit into the essay proper. Don't attempt to stuff in unrelated queries or too many abstract thoughts.

- **Avoid making overblown closing statements.** A conclusion should open up your highly specific, focused discussion, but it should do so without drawing a sweeping lesson about life or human nature. Making such observations may be part of the point of reading, but it's almost always a mistake in essays, where these observations tend to sound overly dramatic or simply silly.

A+ ESSAY CHECKLIST

Congratulations! If you've followed all the steps we've outlined above, you should have a solid literary essay to show for all your efforts. What if you've got your sights set on an A+? To write the kind of superlative essay that will be rewarded with a perfect grade, keep the following rubric in mind. These are the qualities that teachers expect to see in a truly A+ essay. How does yours stack up?

- ✓ Demonstrates a thorough understanding of the book
- ✓ Presents an original, compelling argument
- ✓ Thoughtfully analyzes the text's formal elements
- ✓ Uses appropriate and insightful examples
- ✓ Structures ideas in a logical and progressive order
- ✓ Demonstrates a mastery of sentence construction, transitions, grammar, spelling, and word choice

Suggested Essay Topics

1.   Describe Winston's character as it relates to his attitude
     toward the Party. In what ways might his fatalistic streak
     contribute to his ultimate downfall?

2.   Discuss the idea of Room 101, the place where everyone
     meets his or her worst fear. Keeping in mind that for most
     of Winston's time at the Ministry of Love, he does not
     know what he will find in Room 101, what role does that
     uncertainty play in making Room 101 frightening? Does the
     cage of rats break Winston's spirit, or does it merely play a
     symbolic role?

3.   What role does Big Brother play within the novel? What
     effect does he have on Winston? Is Winston's obsession with
     Big Brother fundamentally similar to or different from his
     obsession with O'Brien?

A+ Student Essay

> How does technology affect the Party's ability to control its
> citizens? In what ways does the Party employ technology
> throughout the novel?

Of the many iconic phrases and ideas to emerge from Orwell's *1984*,
perhaps the most famous is the frightening political slogan "Big
Brother is watching." Many readers think of *1984* as a dystopia
about a populace constantly monitored by technologically advanced
rulers. Yet in truth, the technological tools pale in comparison to the
psychological methods the Party wields, which not only control the
citizens but also teach them to control themselves.

To be sure, the Party uses technology in scary and effective ways.
Its most notable technological weapon is the telescreen, a kind of
two-way television that watches you as you watch it. Telescreens
literalize the idea that Big Brother, the mysterious figure who represents the Party's power and authority, is always watching the
people of Airstrip One. Even the citizens' most mundane actions
are monitored by the telescreens, which must remain turned on at
all times. When Winston performs his Physical Jerks exercises, for
example, a voice from the telescreen criticizes his poor effort. When
he is arrested, a voice from the telescreen tells him what's coming.
Another terrifying technology used by the Party is vaporizing, the
means by which the government executes those who displease it.

Yet despite the power of the omnipresent telescreens and the
terror of vaporizing, they are just two among countless methods
of control. And the most powerful methods turn out to be non-
technological in nature. Posters announce the watchfulness of Big
Brother; mandatory daily meetings called Two Minutes of Hate rile
up the citizenry, allowing them to vent their emotions and solidify
their xenophobia; public hangings make examples out of traitors;
physical torture awaits those who commit thought crimes; and
Junior Spies turn in any adults they feel are not sufficiently loyal to
the party, even if those adults are their own parents. None of these
methods involve technology. Instead, they rely on psychological
manipulation. Together, these methods produce a complex mixture
of terror, paranoia, groupthink, and suspicion that keeps the citizens cowed and obedient.

In addition to, and as a result of, these government tactics, the citizens of Oceania are constantly policing themselves. In order to avoid being jailed or vaporized they closely monitor their own actions, second by second. Most citizens would find it unthinkable, for example, to demonstrate such blatant misbehavior as enjoying a torrid love affair, as Winston does. But the citizens go even further than simply regulating their outward behavior: they also monitor their private thoughts. They have been manipulated into believing that any independent cognition is grounds for arrest by the Thought Police, so they try to keep their inward selves as loyal and unthinking as their outward actions. Because they have been conditioned since birth to accept whatever the Party identifies as truth, they are also able to use doublethink, a method of believing absurd contradictions such as "war is peace." Again, self-policing and doublethink involve no technology beyond the human brain, but they are perhaps the most effective means of control available to the Party.

The Party maintains power primarily through the use of psychology, not technology. We get the sense that if no technology existed, the Party would find equally effective ways of controlling the populace. Orwell wants to warn us against more than the power of technology; he wants to suggest that the human mind is the most dangerous and advanced weapon of all, and that we should never underestimate the ability of people to control each other—and themselves.

GLOSSARY OF LITERARY TERMS

ANTAGONIST

The entity that acts to frustrate the goals of the *protagonist*. The antagonist is usually another *character* but may also be a non-human force.

ANTIHERO / ANTIHEROINE

A *protagonist* who is not admirable or who challenges notions of what should be considered admirable.

CHARACTER

A person, animal, or any other thing with a personality that appears in a *narrative*.

CLIMAX

The moment of greatest intensity in a text or the major turning point in the *plot*.

CONFLICT

The central struggle that moves the *plot* forward. The conflict can be the *protagonist*'s struggle against fate, nature, society, or another person.

FIRST-PERSON POINT OF VIEW

A literary style in which the *narrator* tells the story from his or her own *point of view* and refers to himself or herself as "I." The narrator may be an active participant in the story or just an observer.

HERO / HEROINE

The principal *character* in a literary work or *narrative*.

IMAGERY

Language that brings to mind sense-impressions, representing things that can be seen, smelled, heard, tasted, or touched.

MOTIF

A recurring idea, structure, contrast, or device that develops or informs the major *themes* of a work of literature.

NARRATIVE

A story.

LITERARY ANALYSIS

NARRATOR

The person (sometimes a *character*) who tells a story; the *voice* assumed by the writer. The narrator and the author of the work of literature are not the same person.

PLOT

The arrangement of the events in a story, including the sequence in which they are told, the relative emphasis they are given, and the causal connections between events.

POINT OF VIEW

The *perspective* that a *narrative* takes toward the events it describes.

PROTAGONIST

The main *character* around whom the story revolves.

SETTING

The location of a *narrative* in time and space. Setting creates mood or atmosphere.

SUBPLOT

A secondary *plot* that is of less importance to the overall story but may serve as a point of contrast or comparison to the main plot.

SYMBOL

An object, *character,* figure, or color that is used to represent an abstract idea or concept. Unlike an *emblem*, a symbol may have different meanings in different contexts.

SYNTAX

The way the words in a piece of writing are put together to form lines, phrases, or clauses; the basic structure of a piece of writing.

THEME

A fundamental and universal idea explored in a literary work.

TONE

The author's attitude toward the subject or *characters* of a story or poem or toward the reader.

VOICE

An author's individual way of using language to reflect his or her own personality and attitudes. An author communicates voice through *tone, diction,* and *syntax*.

LITERARY ANALYSIS

A Note on Plagiarism

Plagiarism—presenting someone else's work as your own—rears its ugly head in many forms. Many students know that copying text without citing it is unacceptable. But some don't realize that even if you're not quoting directly, but instead are paraphrasing or summarizing, *it is plagiarism* unless you cite the source.

Here are the most common forms of plagiarism:

- Using an author's phrases, sentences, or paragraphs without citing the source
- Paraphrasing an author's ideas without citing the source
- Passing off another student's work as your own

How do you steer clear of plagiarism? You should *always* acknowledge all words and ideas that aren't your own by using quotation marks around verbatim text or citations like footnotes and endnotes to note another writer's ideas. For more information on how to give credit when credit is due, ask your teacher for guidance or visit www.sparknotes.com.

LITERARY ANALYSIS

REVIEW & RESOURCES

QUIZ

1. How old is Julia?

   A. 26
   B. 30
   C. 32
   D. 35

2. Winston commits thoughtcrime by writing which of the following in his diary?

   A. I HATE BIG BROTHER
   B. DOWN WITH THE PARTY
   C. DOWN WITH BIG BROTHER
   D. DEATH TO BIG BROTHER

3. What piece of evidence of the Party's dishonesty does Winston remember having coming across several years earlier?

   A. A diary containing O'Brien's secret confession that Big Brother does not exist
   B. A videotape from a telescreen showing Inner Party members burning historical documents
   C. A tape-recorded conversation of Emmanuel Goldstein admitting that he is a Party operative, not a Party enemy
   D. A photograph proving that certain individuals were out of the country when they were allegedly committing a crime

4. What organization urges children to turn their parents over to the authorities?

   A. The Party Youth
   B. The Junior Spies
   C. The Outer Party
   D. The Committee of Oceanian Patriotism

5. The psychological principle that allows an individual to believe contradictory ideas at the same time is called what?

   A. Doublemind
   B. Thoughtcrime
   C. Doublethink
   D. Doublespeak

6. Who really wrote the manifesto that O'Brien gives to Winston?

   A. Emmanuel Goldstein
   B. Big Brother
   C. Ayn Rand
   D. O'Brien

7. What does O'Brien use to torture Winston in Room 101?

   A. A cage full of rats
   B. A laser heat machine
   C. A machine that causes full-body physical pain
   D. Hallucinogenic drugs

8. Where do Winston and Julia make love for the first time?

   A. The room above the antiques shop
   B. The forest
   C. Trafalgar Square
   D. The beach

9. What is the last line of the St. Clement's Church song?

   A. Here comes the Party, dear Winston, you're dead!
   B. Here comes Big Brother to step on your shoe!
   C. Until the mousetrap goes snap! on your head!
   D. Here comes a chopper to chop off your head!

10. What does Winston trace in the dust on the table at the end of the novel?

    A. 2 + 2 = 5
    B. I love Big Brother
    C. I love Julia
    D. O'Brien

11. How many times does Julia claim to have had sex with Party members?

    A. 2
    B. 10
    C. Scores
    D. Hundreds

12. Which of the following characters is secretly a member of the Thought Police?

    A. Winston
    B. Mr. Charrington
    C. Syme
    D. Julia

13. What happens to the glass paperweight?

    A. It is confiscated by the Thought Police.
    B. Julia hides it under the mattress.
    C. O'Brien flings it out the window.
    D. It is shattered on the floor.

14. Where is the telescreen hidden in the room above Mr. Charrington's shop?

    A. Behind the picture of St. Clement's
    B. Under the bed
    C. Behind the light fixture
    D. Behind the poster of Big Brother

15. What is the name for the mass rally held every day?

   A. The Two Minutes Rage
   B. The Ten Minutes Hate
   C. The Two Minutes Hate
   D. The Daily Rage

16. Besides Oceania, what are the two countries that make up the rest of the Earth?

   A. Eurasia and Australasia
   B. Eurasia and Eastasia
   C. Eastasia and Africasia
   D. Australasia and Americom

17. What project is Syme working on at the beginning of the novel?

   A. A pamphlet on Emmanuel Goldstein
   B. A new slogan for the party
   C. A revision of a children's history book
   D. A Newspeak dictionary

18. Who turns Parsons in to the Thought Police?

   A. His children
   B. Julia
   C. His wife
   D. O'Brien

19. What does O'Brien say when Winston asks if he has been captured?

   A. "I would die before I would let that happen."
   B. "They got me a long time ago."
   C. "I'm afraid so."
   D. "I am one of them."

20. To what organization does Julia belong?

   A. The Junior Spies
   B. The Two Minutes Hate Committee
   C. The Inner Party
   D. The Junior Anti-Sex League

21. Winston has a memory of running away from his mother and sister and stealing what from them?

    A. Chocolate
    B. Clothing
    C. Money
    D. A diary

22. The setting for Winston's fantasy about Julia running toward him naked is

    A. Eastasia
    B. The place where there is no darkness
    C. The Golden Country
    D. Ye Olde Curiosity Shoppe

23. In what nation did Orwell work for the British Imperial Police?

    A. Bangladesh
    B. Zanzibar
    C. Burma
    D. India

24. In what nation was Orwell born?

    A. India
    B. Bangladesh
    C. Zanzibar
    D. Burma

25. What was George Orwell's real name?

    A. Eric Snow
    B. Terrence Buskington
    C. Timothy Sneed
    D. Eric Blair

ANSWER KEY

1: A; 2: C; 3: D; 4: B; 5: C; 6: D; 7: A; 8: B; 9: D; 10: A; 11: C; 12: B;
13: D; 14: A; 15: C; 16: B; 17: D; 18: A; 19: B; 20: D; 21: A; 22: C;
23: C; 24: A; 25: D

Suggestions for Further Reading

COURTOIS, STEPHANE, et al. *The Black Book of Communism: Crimes, Terror, Repression.* Cambridge: Harvard University Press, 1999.

CRICK, BERNARD. *George Orwell: A Life.* Boston: Little, Brown, 1980.

CUSHMAN, THOMAS and JOHN RODDEN, eds. *George Orwell: Into the Twenty-First Century.* Boulder, CO: Paradigm Publishers, 2005.

HITCHENS, CHRISTOPHER. *Why Orwell Matters.* New York: Basic Books, 2003.

KUBAL, DAVID L. *Outside the Whale: George Orwell's Art & Politics.* Notre Dame, IN: University of Notre Dame Press, 1972.

MEYERS, JEFFREY. *Orwell: Wintry Conscience of a Generation.* New York: W. W. Norton & Co., 2000.

NEWSINGER, JOHN. *Orwell's Politics.* New York: Palgrave Macmillan, 2002.

ORWELL, GEORGE. *Animal Farm: A Fairy Story.* New York: Signet Classic, 1996.

———. *Essays.* New York: Random House, 2002.